THE AFRICAN SVELTE

THE AFRICAN SVELTE

INGENIOUS MISSPELLINGS
THAT MAKE SURPRISING SENSE

•••

DANIEL MENAKER
DRAWINGS BY ROZ CHAST
FOREWORD BY BILLY COLLINS

Houghton Mifflin Harcourt
BOSTON   NEW YORK
2016

For information about permission to reproduce selections from
this book, write to trade.permissions@hmhco.com or to Permissions,
Houghton Mifflin Harcourt Publishing Company, 3 Park Avenue,
19th Floor, New York, New York 10016.

www.hmhco.com

Library of Congress Cataloging-in-Publication Data is available.
ISBN 978-0-544-80063-2

Book design by Martha Kennedy

Printed in the United States of America
DOC 10 9 8 7 6 5 4 3 2 1

FOR KATHERINE,

with gratitude, admiration, and love

There is such a thing as the poetry of a mistake.

— CHARLES BAXTER

FOREWORD, MARCH!

THE FIRST TIME I was aware of Dan Menaker's devotion to the fine points of language was in one of our early conversations, when he credited his mother (as he does in this very book) for his fascination with correctness and even more so with incorrectness. An esteemed magazine editor herself, Mary Grace was intolerant of improper usage to the point where she would cringe at any reference to "Tiffany's." The name of the store, she would remind the offender, was "Tiffany." No possessive. My reaction to Menaker's anecdote was a mixture of respect and amusement at such exactitude, colored by my shame at having said and probably written "Tiffany's" for decades. Like other unaware people, I suspect, I was misled by Truman Capote's memorably titled *Breakfast at Tiffany's,* an example of a phenomenon where a more popular usage replaces the proper, and in this case I mean proper, name. It's just the kind of fine point of usage that must have inspired Dan to compile this collection of verbal clashes.

The type of misusage that preoccupies *The African Svelte* is the erroneous, unconscious confusion caused by some of the many homophones, eggcorns, and malapropisms that complicate our language: waiver/waver, gall/Gaul, derrière/dairy air/Derry air. You get the picture. All of us, it's safe to say, have come across such mistakes in everyday life, handwritten signs in store windows being a rich source. I think what makes these errors interesting is our reaction to them. It's one thing to notice a wrong choice among "their," "there," and "they're," and quite another to be stopped in one's reading or tracks by a reference to the "windshield factor" for "windchill factor."

Because such slips require a little double take on our part, they usually have a humorous effect on us, maybe for the same reason we laugh at jokes. In his book on the effect of jokes on the unconscious, Freud claims that we laugh at jokes because we perceive an incongruity, a moment of illogic that then creates—you guessed it— anxiety. Our laughter, for Freud, is an effort to cover our unease. Maybe if Freud had included some funny jokes instead of the German groaners he offers as examples, he wouldn't force us to approach the mechanics of humor with such deadly seriousness.

Leavening the sense of inaptness in some of these odd couples is a remarkable and, of course, unintended kinship. To say of a relationship that one person controlled the other "like a puppy on a string" is wrong, but by an odd logic we recognize that in order to walk a puppy, a string might be more fitting than a leash. Many of Menaker's pairings seem chosen for this kind of bonus.

A less Freudian reading of why we react the way we

do to the kinds of errors that this book is all about would point out the disparity between hearing words and seeing them on the page, between listening and reading. Mistakes like "to pass mustard" and "dead wringers" are surely committed by people whose experience of English is more auditory than literary. It's the gap between those two spheres that we fall into when confronted with an error as brilliant as a "pillow of strength." We are dealing with errors in translation not from one language to another but from the ear to the eye.

Words can trip us up in many ways. Deconstruction theory claims that we are always hopelessly and pointlessly tangled in the means of our own expression. Here, Dan Menaker, with a sharp ear, a keen eye, and a healthy penchant for elaboration, has isolated a particular source of verbal confusion. His catalog of slip-ups, complete with whimsical, freewheeling commentary, will appeal to anyone with a sense of humor, a taste for the absurd, and an affection for the author's favorite language.

BILLY COLLINS

INTRODUCTION: FROM THERE TO HERE

Or: *The Journey to the African Svelte*

THIS HAPPENED MORE than sixty-five years ago, in the "Tens" at the Little Red Schoolhouse in Greenwich Village. Our teacher, Mabel, asked if anyone knew the names of the three ships in which Columbus and his men sailed to America. We were sitting around in a circle, just talking, which is what we did most of the time. (The school must have hoped it was grooming the Marxist dialecticians of the next generation.) A little girl raised her hand and said, "The Atchison, Topeka, and the Santa Fe."

I went home and told my parents about this exchange. My mother encouraged me to write a letter about what happened and send it to *The New Yorker*. Under the title "Westward Ho," my letter about the incident became an anonymous Talk of the Town piece:

A fourth-grade young lady at The Little Red Schoolhouse was quick with her answer the other day when she was asked to name the ships of Columbus's fleet, we are advised. "Atchison, Topeka, & Santa Fe," she said confidently.

I was (sort of) published in *The New Yorker* at the age of ten! The magazine sent me fifty dollars, and the next day I went to school and gave twenty-five of them to the little girl. She was, after all, the means of production.

In the ensuing half century, writing, editing, copy editing, verbal irony (that addiction), and listening closely to conversation—my own and others'—have taught me that words sometimes speak louder than actions, that they often break more bones than sticks and stones, and that all language is radically metaphorical—representational of reality. All except the most rudimentary language, like "mmm" and "wow." The word "macaroni" isn't macaroni. That is, the word is, obviously, nothing less than but also nothing more than a written or spoken *symbol* of the pasta. So you could say, and I am in fact saying, that words by their very nature are themselves metaphors—our linguistic carryings-over from the mute world.

My attention to words in turn largely degenerated, for too long, into a sense of superiority about speech and writing. Reading the slush pile at *The New Yorker* became a source not only of amusement but of hauteur. Mainly out of this kind of snootery, I began to keep a list of funny mistakes I came across while slogging through the pages of the "fiction stories," as the hopeful submitters sometimes called them. "The zebras were grazing on the African svelte" was the one that started me on this list, because it was itself, in a way, so . . . so *svelte*.

Thus the title of this book. What is, at least figuratively, svelter than the African veldt? What is smoother, from a distance—more understated, more lissome? Despite my discreditable condescension, on a more decent level, I recognized the "correctness," the rightness, of this mistake.

Eventually, various kinds of professional and personal humblings began to dissolve my arrogance. Meanwhile, the better specimens of slush-pile mistakes, which I had begun to think of categorically as "sveltes," kept coming across my desk, at the very earliest stage of their development into what I now view as a collection of beauty and poetry. All of them had that same kind of rightness about them that in many cases equaled and in some cases superseded their wrongnesses.

That is, the funniest of these errors were funny not only because they were errors—the verbal equivalent of trying to put a shoe on the wrong foot—but because even as wrong shoes for the wrong feet, they somehow fit anyway. If you think about them, they give you the same kind of smile you get when you realize you can use the curved handle of a cabinet drawer as a bottle opener, or a nail clipper as a wire cutter, or a car's headlights as outdoor spotlights. It's the comprehension, often unconscious, that every thought our minds produce is connected to every other. It's a species of delight.

Along these same lines of connectivity, I found myself one day reminiscing about the Atchison, Topeka, and the Santa Fe incident, and all the Goldenberg's Peanut Chews it afforded me. (There was a pickle stand around the corner from Little Red, on Sixth Avenue — two cents for a pickle, candy for a nickel.) It also occurred to me, vis-à-vis the *Niña,* the *Pinta,* and the *Santa Maria,* that the A, T, & SF's cadence was pretty much right. Both phrases were also emphatically transportational. And speaking of "trans-," they both were: one -oceanic, the other almost -continental. Both also had to do with historical firsts. Then, of course, there is also the shared use of "Santa."

That first list of "sveltes" — recorded on that quaint device known as paper — grew to sixty, seventy, eighty entries over the course of about ten years. Why "first list"? Reader, I lost it. When *The New Yorker* (where I ended up working for twenty-six years before sitting down at the craps table called book publishing) moved its offices across to the south side of 43rd Street from the north side, the list went missing. The move was chaotic, not least because the staff was allowed to write on the walls, which we did. Some of the messengers used Magic Markers to draw caricatures of editors, some editors did Kilroys, some others drew hearts with improbable sweethearts, like "E. B. White ♥ e. e. cummings."

The move also unleashed the inner anarchist from within a staff accustomed to quiet voices, small offices like rabbit warrens, ceremony, and right-justified columns, one after another, cosseted by ads for Mercedeses, entire islands for sale, and fancy or "special" summer camps. We had a series of Guy Fawkes Days of deface-ment and disposal and grimy wardrobes. Edward Koren, the great artist of the cartoons of fuzzy beasts and anx-ious and equally fuzzy people, designed a T-shirt with one of his fuzzmoid creatures in running shoes, carrying a box, over the legend MOVING DAY. I still have a couple of them. What do you think they would fetch on eBay?

Everyone loses something precious at some point. But I bet that few nonwriters know the particular kind of sharp, un-anesthetized-amputation pain of a manuscript —or part of one, or even a writerly list—getting lost. The heart went out of my svelte collecting for a long time, and every time I came across good sveltes in print, I would get a little depressed. They were the linguistic equivalent of old flames, which like most old flames resisted rekindling.

Besides "African svelte," the only survivor in my mem-ory from that first list is "gue," for "goo." The full phrase was "turtly gue." How suave and Francophonic "gue" is! "Goo" suddenly acquires some elegance despite its mean-ing. You can see Charles Boyer waxing his mustache with gue. In fact, the whole phrase was apt: There is, after all, not only mustache but Turtle wax.

Then, in 2011, I expressed my prolonged seriocomic grief about the missing list to a very good friend and bril-liant writer, James Gleick. It happened that Jim shared my affection and admiration for sveltes and kept a mental list of his own. He encouraged me to start re-compiling and to think about making a book out of the phenomenon. The heart crept back into my svelte collecting, partly because the Internet and social media were fattening up the pickings so nicely. Just yesterday, I swear as I write this, I found this on GalleyCat, an e-bulletin about writers and publishing: "Kim Kardashian's book of selfies called Selfish has taken a lot of slack."

In any case, owing to illnesses, great new television shows, and the distraction of the new (and oxymoronic) social media, it has taken me about five years of actual slack to collect the hundred new svelte specimens that follow. I've tried to exclude the deliberate plays on words and argot mistakes and autocorrect hilarities that the Internet has fed us like a mainline of mutagenic Miracle Gro. The process of trying to establish genuine, innocent provenance for sveltes slowed me down, too.

My return to the African svelte brought with it a broader and more philosophical interest in language and all of its mistakes—mistakes that have grown so numerous and variegated in their species that they require an entire taxonomy. Some of the cross-bred verbal fauna most frequently sighted (and cited):

Spoonerism: The transposition of the initial (or other) sounds of two or more words, as in "Moo or war turds."

Malapropism: The amusing and accidental or humorously purposeful substitution of one sound for another, usually in speech, sometimes in writing, as in this proud announcement from Constable Dogberry in Act 3, Scene

5 of *Much Ado About Nothing*: "Our watch, sir, have indeed comprehended two auspicious persons."

Soramimi: The use in one language of song lyrics from another in such a way as to make them sound the same but have (often wildly and hilariously) different meanings. As a somewhat slanted example, the Brazilian children's song "Pula Pula" ("Jump Jump") became a sensation in Romania, with parodic YouTube videos and extensive radio play, because in Romania, the word *pula*, which is relentlessly repeated in the chorus, means "penis."

Hobson-Jobson: A word from a foreign language is transposed into one's own, as in — from Spanish to English — *cucaracha* to "cockroach."

Mumpsimus: The conscious, one might say stubborn, continuation of a mistake in custom or tradition, or, for our purposes, a word or phrase. I said "vallunya" instead of "vanilla" when I was three or four, and in my family the flavor remained "vallunya" for decades. A friend's family calls Starbucks "Tarbucks" for the same, annoyingly cute reason.

Mondegreen: A word or phrase misheard in such a way as to give it a new meaning, as in "José, can you see" ("Oh, say," etc.), "There's a bathroom on the right" (for the chorus of the Creedence Clearwater Revival song "Bad Moon Rising"), and "very close veins" for — take a guess.

The origin of "mondegreen" teaches an interesting lesson about the creative uses of verbal or at least aural adversity. And as an error itself, the word demonstrates the amazing flexibility and inventiveness of the English language, because it has no formal, linguistic etymology, or if it does, its etymology is, on the face of it, based on a mistake. The American writer Sylvia Wright, in her book of essays with the superb title *Get Away from Me with Those Christmas Presents*, came up with the coinage from the memory of her mother reading to her the Scottish ballad "The Bonnie Earl o' Moray," which goes, in part,

> *Ye Highlands and ye Lowlands,*
> *Oh, where hae ye been?*
> *They hae slain the Earl o' Moray*
> *And laid him on the green.*

Wright, when she was a child, had heard "They hae slain the Earl o' Moray / And Lady Mondegreen."

Which makes its own kind of double-homicide sense. The little girl must have thought, Poor Lady Mondegreen, executed surely because of some innocent connection to the doomed old Earl o' Moray. Mrs. Wright wrote, "The point about what I shall hereafter call mondegreens, since no one else has thought up a word for them, is that they are better than the original."

On a more X-rated level of mondegreens than the slaying and laying-on-the-green of the Earl o' Moray, the 1963 song "Louie Louie," by the Kingsmen, has become perhaps history's most notorious—and costly—example of misheard lyrics. According to an NPR report in 2015 (and as reported elsewhere, including the obituary for Jack Ely, the group's lead singer, in the *New York Times,* also in 2015), after a parent's complaint about her child's exposure to the song, the FBI conducted an investigation into what the lyrics were really up to. The official reason given was that they might constitute a violation of the federal law against the interstate transportation of obscene material.

Originally, the song, written by Richard Berry, was a calypso-style plaint describing a sailor's yearning for his sweetheart. But because of the acoustics, or lack of them, in the Kingsmen's recording studio, the words are largely unintelligible—like a Rorschach test that brings out the id in the subject. (One listener heard "She had a rag on, she moved above. / It won't be long, she'll slip it off. / I held her in my arms and then, / And I told her I'd rather lay her again.")

After two years, the FBI concluded that the words, as recorded, were unintelligible. Two years! Your tax dollars at work. But the FBI's final report represents pretty good bureaucracy self-crucifying value for the money, and the imbroglio gave rise, in 2004, to an excellent rock-history book, by *Rolling Stone*'s Dave Marsh: *Louie Louie: The History and Mythology of the World's Most Famous Rock 'n' Roll Song; Including the Full Details of Its Torture & Persecution at the Hands of the Kingsmen, J. Edgar Hoover's FBI, & a Cast of Millions; & Introducing, for the First Time Anywhere, the Actual Dirty Lyrics.*

We are slowly rounding on "here" from "there"—on the list itself from the genesis of the idea. But before we venture onto the open svelte and hunt for examples, one more, overarching, well-documented category of verbal errors demands attention and distinction, and maybe a semi-confession of sveltic incursion, and that is the eggcorn. Most sources agree that an eggcorn (a descriptive name—that is, "eggcorn" for "acorn") is a mistake in spelling or pronunciation that sounds or reads like the correct spelling or pronunciation of the word or phrase being misused and bears an amusing and often fitting relationship to its origin. A group blog called the Language Log, and another, the Eggcorn Forum—which is among the funniest, most thoughtful, and most authoritative examples of Internet verbal-error sites—list subgroups of language errors, almost to the point of emulating particle physics, with its never-ending supply of new tinynesses, each importantly different from the other. You can come up with new terms yourself. For example, you could call the inadvertent juxtaposition of two letters, as in "jutxaposition," a "tyop." You could call the mishearing of a single word an "odditory." And you could call "the Atchison, Topeka, and the Santa Fe," for "the *Niña,* the *Pinta,* and the *Santa Maria,*" a "cadencia."

There appears to be some mystery about the exact boundaries of the category eggcorn, which leads me to the re-acknowledgment that a svelte should probably be best classified as a species of the genus eggcorn—an eggcorn that has to appear in print. Or put it this way: I haven't seen any definitions of "eggcorn" that specifically *exclude* conversation. That is, the same mistake may also be conversational, but if it's just conversational, as many are, it's an eggcorn but not a sveltic one. You must be able to see the svelte with your own reading eyes, not just hear it with your own hearing ears. You may miss a svelte in conversation, so then it's not a svelte. You can't miss it in print or pixels (unless you think it's correct, of course).

Sveltes must not only be written and make the same kind of funny sense that all eggcorns make; they should also, at least in my book, and so in this book, be in some way aesthetically, often visually, even philosophically pleasing to the mind's eye and the eye's mind. They must themselves be svelte—neat, trim, stylish, and with the elegant sleekness of literally poetic justice.

The sveltes presented in these pages come from books, magazines, signs, flyers, and, most abundantly, the Internet. They were all caught by me or brought in by others from the wild. None were farmed, and they were homegrown only when I accidentally planted them myself. During the admittedly informal process of their collection, some sources have gone missing—gotten lost in the mists of . . . thyme. So you'll have to take the genuineness of their outside provenance on faith. I've tried to bring as much rigor to this project as any sincere graduate-school dropout could muster, but this is not a work of scholarship. To have made it one would have crushed its spirit.

Back for an introductorily final thought about the Internet. As mentioned earlier, the rise of the web has brought with it an exponential proliferation of public—technically, published—texts. This has in turn put svelte production into overdrive. Along with and trafficking in other argots, like rap lyrics and techspeak, the Internet has also at least indirectly fostered a rich—over-rich—culture of linguistic improv. Slang, abbreviations, special vocabularies flow into the mainstream much more easily and quickly now than they used to, swelling it to flood stage. So you will see the Internet as the provenance for many sveltes here—a blessing, for discovery, but a kind of curse against the specialness of this kind of mistake. The more common the coin, the less valuable. I have tried to use as many traditional written sources as I could in compiling this list, but pixels are constantly gaining on print.

In general, not just in svelteland, the balance in the age-old, healthy, and creative conflict between "proper" English and "bad" grammar and spelling and pronunciation has shifted, at least slightly, to the anarchists. So I confess that the spirit behind this book partakes a little of nostalgia—for a time when "for all intensive purposes" and "who are you having lunch with?" and "girlz" could be said to be wrong. Nostalgic laments often amount to not much more than geezer talk, as in, "Why, when I was your age, I had to walk twenty-five miles to school every day, in a blinding snowstorm, even in the summertime, being chased by slavering hyenas, and when I got there, why, you know, there were no pencils, and we had to write with porcupine quills and chicken blood. And, why, the classroom was warmed by the body heat of the mice that were always getting into our lunchboxes, which generally contained a lump of suet, if they contained anything at all."

But maybe it's not completely undiluted geezer talk in this case. Because if you find these sveltes funny, and especially if you agree that the errors possess their own kinds of integrity, you may also experience a pinch of regret about fewer and fewer linguistic bars being held tightly—if only because the increased incidence of sveltes has made each example just a little less like a diamond, than a zircon, in the rough.

THE SVELTES

AS A WEBSITE advises, "You should let the customer know

1. from the gecko

that no creative project has ever finalized as planned."

In Malay, onomatopoeia calls what we call geckos *ge-coqs,* after their vocalizations. There are more kinds of geckos—1,500 species—than of any other lizard, and they have autotomy. That is, they can shed their tails in a pinch, as an appetizer, to throw predators off pursuit of the entrée. They are mainly tropical or subtropical in habitat, have no eyelids, and lick their eyes to keep them moist so as to refresh their color vision, which is 350 times more discriminating than ours. They exude an adhesive substance from their feet and can walk on ceilings, as they often do in tropical climates, where they are regarded fondly, almost like pets, since they eat insects.

The slow pace of the to-me-mystifyingly Cockney-accented gecko who represents the Geico (get it? I just did; embarrassing) insurance company is indeed true to the gecko's ambulation. But attributing bewilderment to him, as the ads often do, is speciesist, implying that he's sort of helpless from the get-go. The ads generally play on the promised speediness of Geico's mantra: "Fifteen minutes could save you fifteen percent or more" on car insurance. The ads, then, and the svelte "gecko" for "get-go," show what we'll see again and again in these kinds of mistakes—a handsome synonymic or antonymic connection between the right and the wrong.

According to some sources, "get-go" started out as an African American slang invention. According to other sources, it is simply a compression, African American or otherwise, of "get going." Others still, a compression of the southern and western idiom "git up and go." In any case, it has caught on everywhere, probably because of its rapid alliteration, which is almost onomatopoetic for an engine starting—onomatopoetic like many other expressions that have a rapid auditory component, like "pitter-pat" and "ah-choo!"

GECKOS LIVE IN HOT, dry climates and unlike sailors do not have bellybuttons, so at least they can't waste their time with what the *Lufkin* (Texas) *Daily News* accused the *New York Times* of—

2. naval gazing.

A QUITE COMMON svelte—"naval" for "navel" and vice versa. The backgrounds of the two words are straightforward and have nothing to do with each other. But you feel —or at least I felt—an immediate instinctive affection for this mistake. The two words are connotative cousins, because what is a navel if not a little ship, afloat on the (sometimes vast) ocean of a tummy? What else is a ship on the ocean if not a micro-omphalos? (Well, OK—many other metaphorical things.) And doesn't naval gazing make sense in its own right? Ask Otis Redding, as he's sittin' on the dock of the bay. Or Ishmael:

> Circumambulate the city of a dreamy Sabbath afternoon. Go from Corlears Hook to Coenties Slip, and from thence, by Whitehall, northward. What do you see?—Posted like silent sentinels all around the town, stand thousands upon thousands of mortal men fixed in ocean reveries. Some leaning against the spiles; some seated upon the pier-heads; some looking over the bulwarks of ships from China; some high aloft in the rigging, as if striving to get a still better seaward peep.

The two kinds of gazing are opposed with regard to distance and focus, but they have in common passive and silent meditation. At the opposite end of the emotional spectrum from meditation, but similarly centered in liquid, is this simple but eloquent sentence from an annoyed email sent by a kid to her mother, right after someone at her summer camp played a water prank of some kind on her:

3. I am sobbing wet.

THERE SEEMS TO be a scholarly consensus that the sound of the word "sob" is probably imitative of some aspect of the act of weeping. And that the same may be true of the words for this grief activity in other languages. This seems strange when, according to *Collins English Dictionary*, these translations include: Czech, *vzlykat;* Danish, *hulke;* Dutch, *snikken;* European Spanish, *sollozar;* German, *schluchzen;* Finnish, *nyyhkyttää.*

It seems far more sensible to transpose "sop" into "sob," given not only their nearly identical sounds but also the serious wetness of both words. It makes similar sense that "sop" shares its derivation with "soup." A sop was originally and still occasionally is a piece of bread or other food to be dipped in soup or sauce. It makes two or three different kinds of sense that the camper came up with this unconfusing confusion.

Campers in distress. I was a counselor for a bunk of eight-year-olds at my uncle's summer camp when I was nineteen. At the beginning, one of the kids in my bunk suffered teasing by the others, because he was seriously unathletic and a little frail-looking. I managed to put an end to the teasing, but not before Greg ran into the bunk alone one day, early in the season, and threw his arms around me, sobbing, over some taunt. Nonplussed, never having found myself *in* this kind of *loco parentis* before, I hugged him and tried my best to comfort him. He calmed down and sat there for a few minutes, and I told him how impressively good he was at some unathletic activity. The sun came out in his face, and he jumped up cheerfully and ran out of the bunk without a word, leaving me with a sobbing-wet T-shirt shoulder, and feeling for the first time in my life something like an adult.

In connection with soup and sopping and sobbing, maybe these first few entries have served to do what a cover letter on a short-story submission was promising to

4. wet your appetite

FOR MORE. (Or maybe the opposite, since "wet" sometimes brings along with it the sense of figurative dampening, as in "wet blanket," or weakness, as in "wet noodle.")

This is a very common svelte, and I join with my wife, Katherine, in finding it not that amusing in itself. But the accidental salivary connotation pleased me for its absolute appropriateness. And the contrast between the images produced in the mind by "whet" and "wet" is a nice sharp one. And don't forget that if you happen to sharpen a tool on a whetstone, you often put oil or water on the blade to keep it from getting too hot. There may also be a confusion in this svelte between the idiomatic whetting of the appetite and the wetting of the whistle.

The metaphorical meaning of "whet"—"to encourage or incite"—appears to have applied to its roots early on. Here, from the invaluable *Online Etymology Dictionary*, is the whole story:

> Old English hwettan "to whet, sharpen," figuratively "incite, encourage," from Proto-Germanic "hwatjan" (cognates: Old Norse "hvetja," "to sharpen, encourage," Middle Low German, Middle Dutch wetten, Old

High German wezzan, German wetzen "to sharpen," Gothic ga-hvatjan "to sharpen, incite"), from PIE [Proto-Indo-European] root *kwed- "to sharpen" (cognates: Sanskrit codati "incites," literally "sharpens"; Old English hwæt "brave, bold," Old Saxon hwat "sharp").

OMG, these etymologies can be so ornate and complex that they can give the reader what an email forwarded to me described as

5. a furled brow.

A FURLED BROW strikes me as a far more dangerous physical and psychological condition than a furrowed one, since "furl" means "to roll or fold up, usually neatly." Think of the forehead of a person in a state of such concern that his brow folds over on itself, maybe more than once, flag-like. He has literally worried himself to death. From the *Online Etymology Dictionary*:

> **furl** *(v.)* 1550s, of uncertain origin, possibly from Middle French *"ferler,"* "to furl," from Old French *"ferlier,"* "chain, tie up, lock away."

A furrow is a thin line in the soil, for planting, or, more figuratively, in the forehead, for thinking. So, as the derivation of "furl" makes clear, the relationship between the two words is closer than one might have at first thought, as furrows are there to plant seeds and lock them away. Both words also imply linearity.

From time to time in my gathering of sveltes, the words brought to mind some real-life experiences that made those words come to life. For the first example, the word "furled" caused a furrowed brow in one of the writers I worked with as a publisher. Matteo Pericoli, a superb Italian artist trained as an architect, created a book called *Manhattan Unfurled,* an elegant foldout, continuous drawing of the entire Manhattan skyline. Matteo was easy to kid, so I kept telling him, "Maybe the title should be *Manhattan Furled,* because when the customer buys it, the drawing is in fact furled."

"Dan, Dan—what are you saying?" Matteo would reply. "It has to be 'unfurled.' That is what is so special, you know."

"I'm not sure. When people buy it, it's definitely furled. Then *they* get to unfurl it."

"Dan, Dan—no, it has to be 'unfurled.'"

"Well, not to be insistent, but would you think about it? You know what 'insistent' means?"

"Yes, Dan, I know what 'insistent' means. My English is very good, you know."

"You are extremely recalcitrant."

"What does this mean?"

Another time, Matteo told me about the wonderful cook and housekeeper who worked for his family. She would serve chicken and boast about the recipe. When she was out of earshot, Matteo's father would say, "Chicken is always chicken."

Cooking and cuisine bring to mind step 3 in an ancient recipe for date candy—

6. Kneed in the walnuts.

OUCH!

You wonder if this is a necessary step in the preparation of whatever cuisine is under discussion. Maybe the author is trying to introduce a personal martial-arts narrative element into his recipes. In any case, "knead" and "kneed" do share a physically vigorous, not to say aggressive, even violent, meaning. So the mistake, as usual, has its own logic and subliminal justice.

"Nuts" for "testicles" started somewhere in the vernacular of the early twentieth century. Who knows whether whoever started it did so because of not only the roughly visual but the definitely reproductive appropriateness of the invention.

"Walnut," in particular, works well both ways. It comes from the Old English *wealhhnutu,* literally "foreign nut," because the tree originated in Persia. You can readily understand why the metaphorical nut of a situation or an idea sits at its center, why the nut is the essential sum of money in a transaction, and why it's that little thing that holds the screw fast. But why does "nut" also mean "crazy person"? Because in the seventeenth century, to be "nutts upon" someone was to be extremely fond of him or her.

That is, to be sort of crazy about, in my case, her. This, in turn, according to etymologists, owed its meaning to the even older slang usage of "nut" for "head."

Haven't you almost gone nuts when you were in what a blog post called

7. the throws of packing?

HOW MANY TIMES have you heard or read something like, "I just threw a lot of things into a suitcase and got to the airport as fast as I could"? Or, I hope not quite as often, "Just throw your stuff together and get out of my house, buster!"

The confusion is etymologically a natural one, because, as is the case with our own origin ("pang of childbirth"), the origins of both words—"throw" and "throe" —include the notion of pain. In fact, it's possible that both words descend from the Old English þrawan, "to curl, writhe." Packing inflicts a certain amount of pain on most of us, unless you are like my late father-in-law, who used to pack two days before a trip and then look on smugly as others scurried around the morning of.

But, then, if "throe" generally connotes pain—as in "death throes"—what do we do with the "throes of passion"? What we do is recognize that we have associated sexual ardor with pain from the beginning. "Hurt so good," as John Mellencamp puts it. So the word can be deployed for two contrasting psychological states, depending on its context.

Most of us pack with both hands, usually on dry land, but the baseball player Pat Venditte, of the Oakland A's, is more adaptable in his work environment, according to the *East Oregonian,* which headlined his first performance this way:

8. Amphibious Pitcher Makes Debut.

BEING ABLE TO operate on land and on or in the water may not seem like a plus for a pitcher, except just before the umpires signal, or at least should signal, for a rain delay—which happens too rarely in these days of televised games—or his team is playing an away game in Atlantis. And Venditte is obviously the go-to reliever if another team pinch-hits Aquaman after climate change makes the movie *Water World* come true.

And what a spitball he can throw!

In Greek, *amphibios* means "leading a double life." (The word "biology" has the same provenance.) It makes sense, then, that baseball experts have long considered lefties and righties to be almost different species, even psychologically. "Ambidextrous," the correct word for the headline, means, on the literal level, "having two right hands," which betrays the ancient prejudice against lefties, as does the word "sinister," which comes from *sinistra*, Latin for "left." The Latin prefix *ambi-* grew out of the Greek *amphi-*. So there's a twoness and a oneness to the roots here.

In other related Greco-Roman words, an amphora was a two-handled vessel for oil and rice and other food supplies. And the second part of the word, "phora," informs "metaphor"—"a carrying over." Which is exactly what the Romans did with the word "amphora" itself—carried it over from Greek.

From the Department of Fussy Losing Battles: We pronounce "amphora" as "amfora," "metaphor" as "metafor," and "amphibious" as "amfibious," so let's please continue—or start, as the case may be—to pronounce "amphitheater" not as "ampitheater" but "amfitheater," and "diphtheria" not as "diptheria" but as "diftheria." Fank you.

But back to our discussion of doubles. A disguise, in a way, makes a person into two people. It creates ambiguity and ambivalence. But there is a disguise that makes a person into no one, as happened when, according to a CNN closed caption,

9. the terrorist was wearing a baklava.

AN UNPRECEDENTED DISGUISE, and in the running for Best Svelte Ever. I wonder how seriously the threats of a terrorist outfitted this way could possibly have been taken. To say nothing of how he managed to sneak a baklava on board a plane through the dessert detector. And exactly where on his terrorist body he was wearing it. But really, it doesn't matter. As long as it alerts us to the danger of passengers at the boarding gate who are sporting sticky, layered pastries.

The word "baklava" probably comes from the Mongolian *bayla*—"to tie, wrap up, pile up." But it gets complicated, because *bayla* is what etymologists call a loanword —from Turkish. In the case of "baklava," with a possibly Persian terminal fragment—the *va*. Just as linguists differ about the origin of the word, Lebanese, Greek, Turkish, Armenian, and other native chefs argue about which of their nations is principally responsible for its culinary invention, but so far without casualties or special ops.

A "balaclava," the haberdashery of choice for many terrorists and no doubt the source of confusion here, is

25

a close-fitting cap that covers the head and neck, leaving only a small part of the face exposed. The word earned its apparel usage at the Battle of Balaclava during the Crimean War. Everything involved here provides an excellent context for an excellent svelte—the region, the violence, the protection, the idea of concealment, and almost all the letters. But, sadly, the opposite of the sweetness.

As long as we're in the neighborhood, and speaking of (arguably) Greek food, another closed-captioner, recording a live spoken report, wrote a few years back,

10. The Russian takeover of Crimea is a feta com plea.

CLOSED CAPTIONS PROVIDE a cornucopia of instant sveltes, and an even bigger supply of garbles, but few of the errors rise to this level of distinction.

Polyphemus, in Book 9 of *The Odyssey*, before making a meal or two of Odysseus's companions, goes about milking his sheep and creating an epic version of feta. Two or three thousand years later, Odysseus's descendants laid European Union legal claim to the term "feta," thus, according to the *Financial Times*, creating an international cheese crisis, which grew out of the economic consequences of Russia's takeover of—guess where! That's right, the Crimea:

> In Brussels . . . negotiators from the EU and the US have been mulling a host of awkward questions as they try to fashion arguably the most ambitious trade pact attempted, [including] whether only Greek producers really should be allowed to sell "feta" cheese.

Before the Greeks', um, plea gave them the exclusive rights to "feta," there was a mighty protest from other nations. As a Cornell University report, "Issues of Regional Identification Involving EU Regulations and 'National' Brands of Food," by Mike Peluso, put it in 2005:

Summary of the Conflict

In 1994, Greece asked for PDO [Protected Designation of Origin] status from the EU for feta cheese, which they contended was a uniquely Greek product. The European Commission accepted this in 1996 despite the anger of Denmark, Germany, and France. These three nations stood to lose a great deal of money if feta became a strictly Greek product. However, this decision was overturned in 1999 due to challenges mounted by the aforementioned nations. The Commission conducted an investigation into the origins of feta, accepting information from both sides, and ... on October 14, 2002 feta cheese was officially named a Greek product that can only be produced in particular areas of Greece and under certain regulations. Other countries have continued to protest this ruling, requiring a recent reaffirmation by the Commission in 2005. The most intriguing development involves the ... entrance into the EU of Bulgaria ... Bulgarians contend that feta is in fact their own, and it appears certain that the feta conflict will continue.

Nevertheless, as of now, no other country's cheese producers in the European Union can call feta "feta." It's a done deal—a *fait accompli*. But evidently not before Bulgaria mounted what a Facebook post called

11. a last-stitch effort.

"LAST DITCH" PROBABLY derives from military sources—the last trench or natural gulley from which to defend against an attack. "Ditch" is a kind of upside-down variant of "dike." That is, in order to build a dike out of soil, you have to dig a ditch. "Stitch," which shares not only its last four letters with "ditch" but also its sense of downward penetration, comes from the Proto-Germanic *stikiz*, for "sting," "stab," or "prick." Sewing's adoption of the modern word is a natural one, then, and "in stitches" shares the painful association of stabbing, however pleasurable the pain.

"Last-stitch effort" may resonate in your mind with phrases like "last straw," "last gasp," "last step," and "last resort," all of which connote exhaustion or surrender or just plain completion. An exhausted seamstress may try to finish the garment she's working on with what she thinks of as a last-stitch effort.

When you've mounted such an effort, you may have to —as a short-story submission put it—

12. undo stress.

"TO UNDO" MEANS not only "to unfasten," say, a button, or "reverse an action that has been taken," but also "to bring to ruin, destroy." As in the fallen maiden's lament, "Alas, I am undone"—in many stagy cases because she has just been . . . done. So "undo stress" would be the anxiety that accompanies the process of being undone. And anxiety is often also "undue"—excessive, not justified by the circumstance that causes it. This is getting too complicated. On to "stress."

The use of the word "stress" in its psychological sense is, believe it or not, only about fifty years old. It still has a faint echo of psychobabble. The therapy industry commandeered it from its meaning of physical pressure or tension.

To really undo stress, we may wish to go where a tweeter said he was during a college lecture—

13. vast asleep.

WHAT IS SLEEP if not, in many ways, vast? Poets are incessantly comparing sleep to oceans, the heavens, death. The past history of the word "vast" also included connotations of desolation and emptiness, and sleep can certainly feel desolate and empty, too. Especially desolate, since that word, at its heart, means "without sun."

And if the tweeter had been fast asleep? "Fast" has many meanings, two of them so opposed that they are striking. "Fixed" and "anchored" vs. "quick," "speedy." Someone has named such words contronyms, and there are dozens of them, and we generally use them without awareness of their contrariness. Think about these and you'll see what I mean: "cleave," "dust," "ravel," "rent," "peer," "splice." Even "handicap," sort of. They remind me of tools that can open or close things, fasten (!) or unfasten, tighten or loosen, pound in or extract, screw and unscrew. Handy.

When we awaken, we may want to have breakfast at what Larry Cooper, the brilliant manuscript editor of this book, told me another book manuscript described as

14. a Grecian spoon.

THERE IS SUCH a thing, eBay (and many other sources) tell us, and you might find it, even greasy, at a greasy spoon: "Oneida 1881 Rogers Silverplate Grecian Spoon Utensil Flatwear Silver Plated." There's also a Grecian fish knife, a Grecian fish fork, a Grecian soup spoon, and a Grecian dessert spoon. The "Grecian" refers to a certain pattern, but I haven't been able to figure out what it is.

"Greasy spoon" is a metonym—the substitution of one term for another of which it is an attribute or aspect or a part—like "the bench" in jurisprudence, "Wall Street," "question mark," "Hollywood." This particular metonymic coinage dates back to the 1920s in America, and many diners and other basic food places now proudly use it as their official name—as others do with "hash house" and "truck stop."

"Grecian Spoon" and "greasy spoon" joined together most memorably in a *Saturday Night Live* skit series in which John Belushi, Dan Aykroyd, and Bill Murray, playing Greek immigrants, ran the cheeburger-Pepsi-and-cheeps–only establishment with the oxymoronically grand name the Olympia Restaurant.

Moving west, from the Crimea earlier, and Greece now, a *New Yorker* receptionist handed the following message to a writer who was just returning from lunch:

15. Al Italia called.

YOU WONDER IF the Italia family was following the example of a Mr. and Mrs. Fields, who according to one source named their son Wrigley, or the four sets of parents who called their kids ESPN, or the British woman who named her daughter Ikea. According to other reports, parents have saddled their offspring with Gouda, Bologna, Xerox, Camry, and many other brand names. And I wonder if and when Mr. Italia was building a house, he had reason to use the services of the Florida construction company Mac Hinery, Inc.

Of course, he might have been calling about his ETA, or maybe he was still up in the air about an assignment for a piece that, as a CNN banner did, asked the question

16. Did Flight MH370 allude radar?

LIKE "LUDICROUS," "PRELUDE," "collude," "post-lude," and maybe even "Quaalude," "allude" and "elude" both have at their hearts *ludere,* Latin for "to play." It also meant "to trick," or "to deceive," and so it makes sense that "allude" and "elude," having largely shed the playful aspect of their beginning, now imply a sense of evasion or indirection. "Allude" is not a transitive verb; you have to allude *to* radar. But that hasn't kept this mistake from proliferating, like flak on a bombing run. You can just hear the cockpit conversation:

PILOT (to copilot): Can you check on that screen thing and tell me if you see anything?

COPILOT: Screen thing?

PILOT: Yeah, you know—that screen with the line that goes around and around.

COPILOT: Line that goes around and around?

PILOT: Yeah, and it shows, like, blips, if there's any traffic. Or flak. At first they're sort of bright, then they fade, and then when the lines hit them again they get bright on the screen again.

COPILOT: Oh—*radar!* That's what you're alluding to. It was eluding me.

And incidentally, "flak" comes from the German *Fliegerabwehrkanone,* or "flyer defense cannon." There is some disagreement about how closely "flack" is related to "flak." Some sources say the lineage is direct, some say "flack" comes at least in part from the name of a movie agent, Gene Flack. And "radar," acronymically, even if roughly so, from "radio detecting and ranging."

The ancients may not have had radar, but they had their own impressive inventions, as we can see from what I myself in writing once referred to as

17. Aztech ruins.

YOU MIGHT THINK that the Aztecs were sort of the opposite of modern technologists and therefore my mistake made a sort of contradictory sense. In fact, I may have made it for that reason—as an unwitting and unconscious play on words. But it's also true that somewhere in the back of my mind I was probably thinking that Aztecs *were* known for various innovations of a technological kind. At least according to the many anthropologists who have marveled at their inventions, mostly involving weapons and agriculture. They used obsidian for arrowheads, apparently a huge step forward over rocks. And they also, as we all know, came up with *atlatls* and *macuahuitls*. The *atlatl* was a kind of propulsive device that effectively lengthened the arm and made it possible to throw spears much faster and farther than they could otherwise be thrown.

There is a World Atlatl Association—yes, there is. It appears to be a very active organization, with publications and competitions and product listings, and a 382-page bibliography of writings about *atlatls*, by John Whittaker of Grinnell College. (When you do research for a book essentially about words, you find yourself almost suffocating in the hypergranularity of human activities and interests.)

Moving on to the *macuahuitl:* It was a nasty weapon with numerous sharp obsidian blades—a ceramic weapon, basically, which looked like a long zucchini with triangular blades studding it longitudinally which severely lacerated its victims (who, you might say, in this way became Aztech ruins). On a website called swordforum.com, a comment reads as follows: "I would definitely be very, very interested in seeing some reasonably scientifically done macuahuitl tests! A pumpkin, a set of pork ribs, and some leather would probably be a reasonable enough approximation of a human torso."

The Aztec calendar was another at least semi-technological invention of these ultimately doomed people. There were actually two Aztec calendars—or "calenders," according to an endearing high-school history project that I found through a Google search. One served as a timekeeper, the other as a reminder of the days to praise gods. This gets complicated. The Aztec life must have been one of perpetual propitiating. The religious calendar had 260 days broken into 20 periods of 13 days each, with each day of each month dedicated to a god. The time calendar had 365 days broken into 18 months, the months consisting of 20 days each. Because natural disasters usually occurred on certain days, five extra days were added to the end of each year—days known as "bad days."

Wait! That makes no sense! Natural disasters do not

usually occur on certain days, do they? Except April 15, but that's an unnatural disaster. Anyway, if babies were born on a bad day, they were named on a good day. Whatever! The time calendar was made of stone and marked with symbols for each day of the month. The symbols were animals, elements, and objects, such as a crocodile, the wind, or a house. The symbols for my personal calendar are my wife Katherine, corn on the cob, Jennifer Lawrence, a log fire, Jane Austen, central air conditioning, our dog Maxwell, a Dutch pillow, popcorn, and bacon. Actually, two days have bacon as their symbol.

Technology and inventions always spawn their own argots, including, used incorrectly, in a

18. calender.

(COULDN'T JUST let that one go.)

"Calender" for "calendar" is a pretty anemic svelte, I realize. At first glance, just a spelling error. But its meaning —a machine consisting of big, pressure-applying rollers that at the end of the paper-making process roll the paper out flat and finished and ready for printing—earns its inclusion here. The mistake in that high-school assignment brings to mind the way the Aztecs in fact made their version of paper, often from pressed tree bark.

Recent technological inventions such as spell check demonstrate how bewilderingly numerous and obscure job-related terminologies, such as "calender," can be—by indicating that they are "incorrect." English is always running ahead of not only printed dictionaries but also such quickly updatable reference sources as spell check and autocorrect. That's what just happened when I typed "calender" into an experimental mono-word Word document. That little wormy red underline appeared immediately.

The word "calender" comes from the Greek *kylindros*, which means "cylinder." What better verbal parentage for a big roller thing? "Calendar" comes from the Latin *calends*—the day of the Roman month when debts fell due—from *calare*, "to announce solemnly, call out." The connection between this kind of public announcement and the rolling out of paper by calenders may be a little tenuous, but both seem to me to have to do with issuance.

As every schoolkid knows, Latin and the culture of Rome have over the centuries exerted a huge influence on modern civilization and its languages. Mix Latin's literary legacy with the also considerable influence of Irish writing and you may get—as mentioned, with all seriousness, in a tweet—a

19. roman o'clay.

THE PHRASE *roman à clef,* Celtically svelted here, once threatened to drag me into court. And did drag me into a deposition. In the flap copy for Anonymous's novel *Primary Colors,* which was about the political campaign of a Bill Clinton–like character, I referred to the book as a *roman à clef*—from the French, "novel with a key." A Harlem school librarian tried to sue Random House and me and Joe Klein (who eventually went nonymous) for libel and invasion of privacy, based on a quickie sex episode starring the fictional candidate and a—well, a Harlem school librarian. The teacher's attorney cited my *roman à clef* description as one of the grounds for the suit.

The suit turned out to have feet o'clay, in large part because the plaintiff was young and black and the character was middle-aged and Jewish. It was eventually dismissed after dragging on for a few years, a sort of literary *Jarndyce v. Jarndyce, Jr.* But, see, this mistake on Twitter does suggest the vulnerability of clay feet—and clay idols, for that matter—which in turn bears on the literary (and sometimes legal) vulnerability of novels *à clef.* Many readers find such stories not really fictive enough to deserve high praise.

(An old joke faintly echoes this svelte: Who is the first Irishman to come out in the spring? Paddy O'Furniture.)

This kind of novel, and autobiographical fiction in general, often receives less aesthetic respect than those works that appear to be more fully imaginative. They shouldn't. Fiction is fiction, no matter how close it sticks to or how far it departs from whatever the author's reality may be. Because, strictly speaking, in order to *be* a novel at all, a story by definition has to be a work of invention. That the experiences and emotional insights and dramatic shape of the events in such works seem close to some writer's personal life doesn't mean the work is less creative than it "should" be. Think of, to name a few: *The Bell Jar, The Fire Next Time, The Blithedale Romance, Buddenbrooks,* and *The Sun Also Rises*—these are all autobiographical and some are even o'clay. And they are also all, of course, great.

In fact, *all* stories, even "true" ones, must use the methods of fiction. The infinite complexity of even the most everyday experiences defies efforts to narrate them with anything like completeness. William Maxwell, my teacher at *The New Yorker,* put it this (provocative) way, in a letter to me: "The minute we begin talking about the past, we begin to lie." An extreme generalization, maybe, but in my opinion true. Because the very process of selection —of imposing form and unity on the chaos and infinite complexity of our lives—misrepresents them, however beautifully and meaningfully, and even usefully.

As with "furled brow," previously, "roman o'clay" brings to mind a real-life conversation that involved some aspect of the svelte under discussion. Roger Angell, another great but thornier teacher at *The New Yorker*, once complained to me about what he saw as the autobiographical nature of stories by two of the magazine's regular contributors. He happened to know that the stories used many elements of the writers' and their families' lives. Out of my own brand of purism, which persists to this day, I said, "But that's because you *know* about their lives. It could be that the stories of a dozen other writers are just as autobiographical but we don't happen to know about them." In this same connection, Roger once complimented me on a novel that I had written, *The Treatment*. He said he thought the book's second half was especially good because it seemed "more made up." By all critical accounts except his, the first half of that book was much better than the second.

And here is another story about a short story that makes this point perfectly. A writer I worked with wrote a piece about a young woman who got involved in a strange and disturbing sexual situation with a rich and isolated older man. She had to perform certain acts that struck me as not only unusual but also very different from any experience the reserved and proper writer could ever have had. That is, the story seemed entirely, and fancifully, made up, in a way that I found surprising and impressive.

After I spoke to the writer on the phone about the suggestions I had for the piece, I said that I thought this story ought to put to rest the idea going around that all her fiction was strictly autobiographical. "Maybe you wrote this one just to show the critics." She didn't say anything. But she giggled a little. I said, "What? Are you saying that this all really . . . ?" More giggles. "Wait," I said, "are you telling me that this story is based—?" She interrupted me with another giggle and said, "Never mind."

As far as the amount of autobiography to be allowed in fiction was concerned, Roger Angell might have cast his vote with those whom the *New York Times* (!) once characterized as

20. no-nothings.

THE FULL SENTENCE, pointed out in the *Times* error blog a couple of years ago, was "A second [candidate] thundered against his party as no-nothings."

The Know-Nothing Party of the mid-nineteenth century, formally the American Party, formerly the Native American Party, got its vernacular name from its initially secretive activities. When a member was asked about them, he was to respond, "I know nothing." (So the nickname did not grow out of the group's advocacy of willful political ignorance, as the name suggests and many believe.) But the mistake of referring to them as "no-nothings" must have come pretty naturally, and even logically, since the party opposed many things—Catholicism, immigration, abolitionism, and, in another branch of the movement, slavery. For a while, the party had considerable electoral success—for example, winning almost complete control of the state government in Massachusetts. But it eventually fell apart, mainly over the issue of emancipation. Some political scientists believe one of its branches proved a forerunner of today's Tea Party.

As with many other historical events and movements and moments, when you begin to read about American politics in the mid-nineteenth century, the texts tend to dispute each other with regard to causes and influences and doctrines. The idea of time travel initially caught on at least in part because it appeared to offer a way of determining what "really happened" in the past. But novelists and moviemakers soon grabbed hold of the concept and turned it into a seemingly endless source of entertainment and combinatorial narratives, such as the one described in this movie-plot summary:

21. . . . in which H. G. Wells builds a time machine which is high jacked by Jack the Ripper.

WHO BETTER?

"Hijack" is a word-derivation goldmine. Some speculate that it comes from "highway jackroller," nineteenth-century slang for a highwayman. Others say it comes from the French *E, Jacques*, a scornful and threatening generic greeting to those unfortunates about to be robbed on the road. Or, somewhat similarly, as a reader would have it in the *Guardian*:

> It originates from the prohibition era in America. Supposedly a member of one gang would approach the driver of a rival gang's bootlegging truck with a smile and a disarming 'Hi, Jack!' before sticking the muzzle of a gat in the face of the poor unfortunate, and relieving him of both truck and its alcoholic cargo. —TIM WOOD, Cardiff

If "hijack" did grow out of "highway" and "jackroller," as seems to me the more likely theory, then "high jack," on the page, has a marvelously antique and appropriate look about it. Also, in popular culture, criminality often includes intoxication of one kind or another, giving us the "high" aspect of this svelte, and the fact that a "jack" is a tool for lifting provides another appropriate element to the mistake. In fact, "jack" serves many other verbal purposes, slangy and more formal, and many of them are working hard in this svelte. Think of the specific, intended anonymity of "jack of all trades," the game aspect of "jacks," the playing card "jack," which is often called the knave, and so on.

More about "jack": Is "Jack" not a nickname for "John"? It is. Why? It's unclear and complicated. The name "Jack" is almost a thousand years old and started out as a generic name for peons. As time went by, "Jack" in this meaning became a glue-on, as in "lumberjack," "steeplejack," and, yes, "jackass." "John" was also a long-standing nickname for male ordinaries, thus "John Doe," and the designation of a prostitute's customer—a "john." This could explain how the John-Jack thing happened. Or the coinage may have been struck by the Normans' "John" equivalent, "Jen." Like us all, the Normans relentlessly diminutivized. Jen became Jenkin and then Jakin, who probably became Jack. There are similarly elaborate explanations of Margaret into Peggy, Richard into Dick, Charles into Chuck, and Sarah into Sally.

At this tipsy point in my evening's writing session, "high jack" reminds me of the folk myth of High John the Conqueror, a sexual superman/trickster, as well as the botanical/aphrodisiacal named after him, High John the Conqueror root. According to legend, High John the Conqueror was a former African prince taken in slavery but with an unbreakable spirit, and he had a magical, er, root. In his subprimal song "I'm a Man," Ellas McDaniel (aka—and usually ka—Bo Diddley) promises to go down to "Kansas Stew" (beats me) and return with his second cousin, whom he calls Little Johnny the cocheroo. Though in other transcriptions it's "Little Johnny the Concheroo" and "Johnny Conqueroo."

Of the hero she calls "High John de Conquer," Zora Neale Hurston writes:

> He is not dead. He waits to return when his people shall call him again ... High John de Conquer went back to Africa, but he left his power here, and placed his American dwelling in the root of a certain plant. Only possess that root, and he can be summoned at any time.

The plant referred to by "conqueror root" is *Ipomoea jalapa*. Its dried tubers resemble testicles and are carried in red flannel bags, called mojo bags. When rubbed, the conqueror root tubers bring good luck in gambling and seduction. (I'm happy to tell you that Willie Dixon wrote and recorded a song called "Rub My Root.")

Hijackers' victims surely suffer what a previous svelter

called "undo stress." But many criminals must also often experience it, owing to the anxiety that accompanies most of their work—pimps in particular, as their job, which involves not jacks but johns, consists mainly of managing undone women. In fact, according to a tweet a friend came across and sent to me,

22. Pimps feel they get a bad wrap, arent at all like sex traffickers ie, the international shit, holding bitches hostage.

THE EXAMPLE PROBABLY should have ended with its sweet little svelte, "wrap," but the rest of the sentence struck me as too eloquent and plaintive, in its conveying of pimp indignation, to leave out.

"Pimp" probably comes from the French *pimper*, "to dress elegantly." So when pimps, who dress with their own version of elegance, get a bad wrap of international shit, it must be particularly discouraging. The papery phrase "rap sheet" goes nicely with "bad wrap," and "that's a wrap"—the movie term for the end of shooting a scene —evokes a suddenness of termination which resonates with "rap."

"Rap," like "jack" and many other short, staccato words —"smack," "block," "stop," "bit," "cut," etc.—has multiple meanings. In the case of "rap," many of those meanings appear to have originated with the definition "a light blow" (noun) or "to hit briefly" (verb). It has also signified a light and improvisational form of conversation, which meaning has evolved into a kind of music whose lyrics are spoken to a beat. These lyrics often have a transgressive element, describing activities that sometimes end up briefly designated on a rap sheet.

The criminal connotation of "rap" puts me in mind of a Twitter feed someone sent me, citing

23. #MarshalLaw.

IS THE HASHTAG "MarshalLaw" a svelte for "Martial-Law"? Or not? I hope not—I hope there's a tweeting lawyer out there who is, however lamely, purposely, maybe even purposefully, punning on his own name. Or invoking, e.g., E. G., Supreme Court Justice Thurgood, Supreme Court Justice John, or Penny Marshall. But, then, I also hope it *is* a sveltic error, because the adjective "martial" and the verb "to marshal" go so well together.

You originally marshaled horses—put them in order—so that they would be ready to fight. And "martial" derives from Mars, the Roman god of war, which is why it has come to be used in reference to not only a kind of law but also a kind of music, certain arts, and courts. So, as to the proximity of "martial" to "marshal"—Viola!, as I used to mispronounce to myself when I was nine or ten.

Finally, "marshal" comes from the Old French word *mareschal*—"a high officer in the royal court"—so even though these two words come from different families, they are brothers.

As noted, #MarshalLaw may be a punster rather than a svelte committer, puns being another aural—but deliberate—equivalent, or at least a cousin, of svelte. Theories about the humor-inferiority and groan-inducement of punning are numerous, one neurological explanation asserting that puns actually inflict a kind of nerve pain in the listener. Knock-knock jokes generally take the form of formalized, non-spontaneous puns. The best one I ever heard is:

"Knock-knock."
"Who's there?"
"Eskimos, Christians, and Italians."
"Eskimos, Christians, and Italians who?"
"Eskimos Christians, and Italians no lies."

If #MarshalLaw is accidental, it raises the matter of mistakes like "calender" and "wet your appetite," which are quieter and more subtle—and therefore usually less overtly funny—than, say, "feta com plea" and "roman o'clay." For some reason that I don't understand, a lot of these less hilarious examples show most clearly the close relationship between the mistake and the right word or phrase.

Another subtle svelte occurs in Dana Spiotta's very good novel *Stone Arabia*, which describes a

24. song-cycle [that] seems to waiver from quiet to intense.

"WAIVER" AND "WAVER" live very close to each other on Option Street, in Maybe City, Alternative County. They both have meanings that involve decision-making. "Waiver" probably comes to us from the Old French *guever*, "to abandon, give back." And "waver" is perhaps connected to the Old English *wæfre*— "restless, wavering."

What is a waif if not abandoned? He is the human embodiment of a right or protection that we give up by signing a waiver. We ourselves become waifs to whatever degree the waiver involved gives up legal protections. The "restlessness" background of "waver" provides a similar kind of texture, as it conveys the notion of physically moving in an uncommitted way from one place to another.

This is one of those particularly poetic sveltes, and one in whose good company I hope my own tweet

25. Grand Budapest Hotel officially joins kale as most noisesomely ubiquitous and overrated phenomenon of 1st Quarter of 2014

MAY BELONG.

"Noisome" descends, fittingly, from the same family as "annoy." *Grand Budapest Hotel* was a noisily ubiquitous movie, as I intended to say, but also noisily annoying, as I ended up saying—advertised and social-mediatized ubiquitously months before its release.

And "noise" may well have its origin in the Latin *nausea* —"disgust or annoyance." So in hindsight it seems strange that "noise" and "noisome" haven't fallen from the same family tree.

Maybe svelting runs in the family. When my son, Will, wrote about Henry VIII for middle-school homework many years ago, he identified one of the king's many wives, and the mother of Elizabeth I, as

26. Amber Lynn.

HOW PERFECT IS THIS, since Amber Lynn is the name of a former award-winning porn star—*I've been told*—and Anne Boleyn herself lived a sexually complicated, or at least vexed, existence. (If today's Amber Lynn has sinned, she has not paid for it with her life, thank goodness, and, according to a profile in the *Los Angeles Times* and other dispatches, has turned to good works, holding fundraisers for AIDS research and helping drug addicts to recover.)

Anne B. has provided us with another kind of sensationalism. Her guilt or innocence has given centuries' worth of scholars and novelists—of late, particularly Hilary Mantel—something to write and write and *write* about. Literary historians say that Anne may also be the primary subject/suspect of one of my Top Ten Poems, by her (perhaps) lover, Sir Thomas Wyatt.

They Flee from Me

They flee from me that sometime did me seek
With naked foot, stalking in my chamber.
I have seen them gentle, tame, and meek,

That now are wild and do not remember
That sometime they put themself in danger
To take bread at my hand; and now they range,
Busily seeking with a continual change.

Thanked be fortune it hath been otherwise
Twenty times better; but once in special,
In thin array after a pleasant guise,
When her loose gown from her shoulders did fall,
And she me caught in her arms long and small;
Therewithall sweetly did me kiss
And softly said, "Dear heart, how like you this?"

It was no dream: I lay broad waking.
But all is turned thorough my gentleness
Into a strange fashion of forsaking;
And I have leave to go of her goodness,
And she also, to use newfangleness.
But since that I so kindly am served
I would fain know what she hath deserved.

The "fang" in Wyatt's "newfangleness" indeed refers back, ultimately, to an animal's fang—a catching tooth, which fixes prey. Its first ancestor is probably the Proto-Indo-European *pag-*, "to make firm, to fix or fasten," which probably also went along a different branch to produce the Latin word *pax*.

Fang. Peace. Go figure. Well, thank you—someone *has* gone and figured, and this is what he says about the apparent paradox:

> But what could possibly be "fastening" about peace? Take the word *pact*, another term relating to conflict studies and a descendant of the same root. A pact is an agreement, a negotiation, which binds together two parties. In light of its etymology, we might think of *peace* not merely as a state, but as an action, that of binding ourselves together firmly and fixedly, through words. Peace, then, can be seen as a performance of language, and it takes work to fasten the agreement, and to keep it fastened.
>
> —JOHN KELLY, on the website
> languageinconflict.org, September 16, 2013

Fang. Wyatt's chamber in "They Flee from Me" is a metaphorical forest, complete with hunters and game. But no warden. Look at not only "new*fang*leness" but "stalking" and "dear heart" ("deer hart"), "tame," "wild," "range." And birds are flying around in there, too, to "take bread" at the poet's hand. So we have romance as a hunt, a taming, and then a fleeing. Hmmm. Love, like the word "fang," is at once violent and affectionate, fastening and wounding.

The word "danger," like "fang," also works in two contrary ways. "Danger" means, well, "danger," as we think of it. But in Wyatt's day, it also referred to the power or control of a lord and master. So someone who has put himself or herself in danger could actually be under the *protection* of a more powerful person.

Wyatt is said to have borrowed "newfangleness" from Chaucer's use of the word. It occurs in "The Knight's Tale":

Men loven of propre kynde newefangelnesse,
As briddes doon, that men in cages fede,
For though thou nyght and day take of hem hede,
And strawe hir cage faire and softe as silk,
And yeve hem sugre, hony, breed, and milk,
Yet right anon as that his dore is uppe,
He with his feet wol spurne adoun his cuppe,
And to the wode he wole and wormes ete.

Rough translation

We love new and different things, like birds we keep and feed in cages which, no matter how luxurious their lives and no matter how carefully we tend to them and give them food and sweets, will fly away to the woods when the cage door is open, and eat worms.

Wyatt was a great scholar—he invented the English sonnet form, among many other literary newfanglednesses. So of course he would have known how closely he was basing his poem on Chaucer's knight's reflection on a lover's fickleness. Especially that "take bread at my hand" bit. Tsk. Close. Wyatt was tall and handsome, too, and a courtier to Elizabeth I. Henry VIII imprisoned him, along with four or five others whom he accused of adultery with "Amber Lynn." But Thomas Cromwell, the Machiavelli of England, saw to it that Wyatt alone was spared execution.

Thank God for royalty, is what writers ought to do. Really. Solomon, Herod, Hrothgar (*Beowulf*) , Arthur, all the Henrys, Richards, and Marys, Elizabeth, Rainier, Amber Lynn—what literary treasures writers have found in their stories! Just talk once again to Hilary Mantel.

Kings and queens play so many major roles in literature, paradoxically, because, of course, stories about them demonstrate and magnify the fact that every human being is, well, human. Stories about ordinary people—Job, Everyman, *The Grapes of Wrath*, um, *Ordinary People*—do exactly the same things from a reverse direction. Willy Loman's quotidian trials become emblematic of the human condition and a certain nobility, however pathetic. The pity and terror inflicted by destiny and the gods and poor character, the good fortune of high birth, wealth, and virtue—these warring factions who live so close to each other form the conflicted nation of drama and narrative and poetry. That the language which presents them to us itself falls victim to and benefits from paradox, tension, and error only makes sense. Even the word "king" has a pearl of paradox in its crown; it's kin to "kin."

In the olden days, kings had jesters. To fill this role, they surely had to be what a Facebook post calls

27. fool hearty.

ONE OF THE DEFINITIONS in the *Urban Dictionary* says that "fool" is "a term for friend or buddy which is mostly used by non-white ethnicities, as in, 'Hey, fool, you wanna play some basketball?'" This affectionate modern vernacular usage sweetly echoes the archaic use of "fool" for "baby." As when Polonius punningly warns Ophelia that if she is too intimate with Hamlet, she "will tender" her father "a fool."

"Hearty" and "hardy" have so many resemblances as to make this mistake almost not a mistake. Both adjectives apply to foods, for example, and often the same foods. And to be a hardy fool would seem to require being a hearty one.

Most of us do our most physically foolhardy things in childhood and adolescence. Or used to, before terrorism and less stoic views of young lives made adults try to safeguard their kids ever more strictly. Maybe this is, or was, nature's tragic way of winnowing out the population, though the tragedies that sometimes result from young stunts don't often bring to mind Darwinian selectivity.

We used to ride on the running board of my uncle's old station wagon and yell to him, "Brush me, brush me!"

so that he would drive on the side of the road and brush us up against the hedges and bushes there. Ride on the backs of pickups with our legs dangling off the back. In college once, I rode home drunk while lying on my back on the sloping trunk of the Porsche owned by a rich kid, and every time he took a curve, I would slide this way or that, like a windshield wiper set on "random," and come very close to falling off. Heavy drinking all by itself may weed out the more foolish and reckless genes that assert themselves in adolescence.

"Hardy" involves an exterior kind of hardness—survival against tough weather or other testing, trying outside circumstances. The folk hero/rapscallion John Hardy and the more anodyne Hardy Boys come to mind. Unfortunately, kale and Brussels sprouts are among the hardy botanicals.

"Hearty" suggests interiority—the heart, of course—and has about it a paradoxical kind of vulnerability. Heart vs. hide. "Foolhardy" is also a paradox if you dissect it. Taking foolish risks may put an end to your hardiness.

Foolhardiness frequently characterizes what a *New Yorker* short-story submission referred to as

28. J-walking.

A NIFTY LITTLE SVELTE. You can see a maybe-drunken jaywalker wandering across a busy intersection and then, as in the letter's curlicue at the bottom, wandering back the way he came. There have been more than a few tragic deaths in New York owing to cars hitting people in crosswalks who are crossing with the Walk sign as often as, if not more often than, jaywalkers. One of the best things about New Yorkers is their relentless disregard for lights against walking, if the coast is clear. They are very careful about this, and they sometimes feel that they can actually be safer by jaywalking than by chickenwalking. Chickenwalking involves taking a step out in front of huge squadrons of angry cars lined up at red lights, champing at their grilles to get going. Sort of like the Red Sea vis-à-vis the Egyptians, is the way you feel. Whereas seeing that there are no cars in sight in either direction, even when it's all Don't Walk, you can be safe and canny in crossing.

In a *New Yorker* profile of Ralph Nader, many years ago, the reporter was with Nader at a street crossing in Washington at something like three in the morning, red light glowing, with no cars anywhere, except maybe for one police vehicle a hundred miles away, in Lynchburg. The writer started to cross, and Nader upbraided him for breaking the law. He—and maybe you—would doubt my conviction that jaywalking can be defended, even on grounds of safety, but, then, I ask him, and you, to regard this, from the website Today I Found Out (which I just actually did—find out, I mean):

> The interesting thing about the "safety" factor of crosswalks vs. jaywalking is that it isn't entirely true. As noted in an article a few days ago, recent studies have shown that pedestrians actually are about 28% less likely to be hurt while crossing a street if they jaywalk ... This is thought to be the case because people who jaywalk tend to be more careful when crossing the road than those who are crossing in crosswalks.

There seems to be some disagreement about the origin of "jaywalk." Some say it descends from the impudence and boldness of the jaybird. That would be fine with me. Others say that it comes from a sort of class term, indicating the birdbrained stupidity or drunkenness of the hoi polloi. Snobby. Naturally, the word sprang up around the turn of the last century, in tandem with the springing up and occasional running down of the automobile.

Starting around 1709, "jay" evidently referred to a chatterer or an impudent person, and the word may be onomatopoetic, echoing the jay's call. The blue jay's Latin classification name is as striking as the blue jay itself: *Cya-nocitta cristata*. "Crested blue," more or less.

"J-walking" sounds like a possible Michael Jackson move. Shifting from the feet to their manual partners, in a *New York Times* op-ed-page submission, we behold

29. slight of hand,

AN INCREASINGLY COMMON SVELTE. "Slight" comes from the Old Norse *slettr*, meaning "smooth" or "sleek." So in a way it seconds the etymological motion of "sleight of hand," as the ancestor of "sleight" is also an Old Norse word, *sloegð*, which meant "cleverness" or "cunning."

Sir Thomas Wyatt's "once in especial" mistress was probably slight of hand, having caught him "in her arms long and small." There is something cunning and almost magical about people, especially women, who are slight of hand. We male oven mitts often have to ask for help buttoning a button or threading a needle. In the fourteenth century, "cunning" meant "learned, skillful."

I once wrote a tribute to Harold Brodkey for the *New York Times Book Review*, in which I referred to his "elegant hands," I think because I remembered/imagined that his ornate and articulated sentences must have been written by elegant hands. After the piece ran, his wife, Ellen Brodkey, called me to thank me for it, even though it was in some places critical. "One thing," she said, and I got ready for some criticism myself. Then she sort of laughed and said, "Harold had stubby, unattractive hands. He *hated* his hands."

In that semi-obituary about Brodkey, I wrote that

there were four or five conversational chords that Harold struck repeatedly: his own talent; the possible talent of younger writers who posed no major-league literary threat to him; the basic inferiority of the other big-timers; examples of how unequipped intellectually and esthetically most editors were to work with him and his prose; and, most salient and astonishing of all, the larceny other writers perpetrated with regard to his style — his "sentences," as he often called his writing.

I cite that passage here partly to furnish a transition and partly to show that Harold never suffered from what a high-school student, in an essay, called his own lack of

30. self of steam.

YOU DON'T NEED roots or derivations to appreciate the suitability and inventiveness of this svelte. Especially when you think of such expressions as "build up steam," "lose steam," "head of steam," and "full steam ahead," steam being a metaphor for energy, velocity, even anger (as in "I am really steamed").

Many such basic words as "self" and "steam" don't house metaphors; they both appear to have meant what they mean in their literal senses now in every earlier language from which they journeyed over into English.

I'm guessing that many of those who suffer from low self of steam do so because, to quote a *Washington Post* theater review, they are

31. faux-gentile.

HOW MANY JEWISH PEOPLE, besides (it has been argued) Gatsby, have wanted to pass as gentile? Well, Larry Zeiger decided to be Larry King. Joan Molinsky chose to be Joan Rivers. Charles Buchinsky changed into Charles Bronson. Winona Ryder was Winona Horowitz. Kirk Douglas wanted out of Isadore Demsky. Most ironical of all, because of his insistence on getting at the truth, Jon Stewart used to be Jonathan Stuart Leibowitz.

(According to a number of genealogical sources, Mary Queen of Scots altered the spelling of her name—from Stewart to Stuart—when she lived in France, so that the locals could get the pronunciation right, instead of making the "w" into a "v." In all today, according to the Stuart Baxter Family & Reunion Blog, "There are approximately twenty-four spellings in use: Stiubhard, Stewart, Steward, Stuart, Steuart, Steuard, Steuarde, Sdiuord, Stevarde, Stevarte, Stewerd, Stigeweard, Stiuard, Stiubhart, Stiward, Stuard, Stuarde, Stuarte, Stuerd, Stuward, Styward, Stywarde, Stueart, and Steuardt." But no "Leibowitz.")

For centuries, "gentile," confoundingly, meant, among other confusing things, *non*-Christian. So someone who is "faux-gentile" would *not* be a Christian. Or the opposite.

Would he or she want to change his name to Leibowitz? It's late in the day and I can't parse this one out.

Faux-gentile people may be trying to hide the fact that they—like the down-and-out protagonist of a novel manuscript sent to me—have to

32. eek out a living.

ONCE AGAIN, you don't need anyone to point out how correct this (fairly common) mistake is. This cry of anxiety and alarm fits in nicely with the marginality of those who must eke out their living. "Eek," as onomatopoeia, is shorter and less desperate than such words as "aaagghh" and its variants, and it has no variants, because along with its brevity, comics and novels and closed captions have pretty much settled on it. You don't see "eeek" very often, if at all. But you do see "aaghh" and "aaaagghh" and "aagh" from time to time.

"Eke" has a sweet little paradox in its background, because its antecedents in Old Norse, Danish, Old Frisian, Proto-Indo-European and, for all I know, Indo-Europrotopean, appear to denote, for the most part, "increase" or "augment." Now, for us, it connotes spare resources rather than any sort of overage. The adverb "eke," archaic, meaning "also"—as in *The Two Noble Kinsmen*'s "long tail and eke long tool"—appears to have its roots tangled with the other "eke" in its indication of augmentation. BTW, "spare" itself is a paradox, since it can mean "extra" or "in short supply." (See No. 13 for other contronyms.) It just now occurs to me that the following commits the

79

same svelte in a less abstract and funnier way. It's from an unpublished novel manuscript: "The sound of brakes eeked up from the street below."

At this point in assembling this list, and as a result of doing a great deal of research about word origins and other aspects of language, I began to wonder about broader questions, the subsoil of the African svelte, its plate tectonics, whether in some way the flowers of our words manifest their roots. The "eeking" of brakes seemed like a good place to stop and reflect for a little while about some theories of language that I ran across as I explored the svelte. And so here is this book's first

BRAKE.

MOST OF OUR important words, beyond ejaculations and some basic ones that seem rootless ("jaw," "tantrum," "bad," "big," "dog") — words that seem to have come from nowhere and in their beginnings meant what they meant and not much more — are packed with the past. Like the soil we walk on, most of the words we speak and write hide secret kinds of life, or cover fossil meanings and feelings that may appear to have been lost but are still "in there," like the ingredients in Ragú spaghetti sauce in those television ads of old.

These covert etymologies still affect the import, the shading, of what we say, even if we don't realize it. There is almost no such thing as plain speech. And generally in reading and listening, there is no such thing as simple understanding.

All that is why there are such things as synonyms, the *mot juste*, the gaffe, the clinker, the inadvertent insult, great poetry. And editors.

It's why the title of George Jones's "He Stopped Loving Her Today" isn't "He Ceased Loving Her Today." Why it's not:

- "All happy families are similar,"
- "To exist or not to exist,"
- "Now is the time for all good men to come to the assistance of the party,"
- "You can't get to that place from this one,"
- "A stitch in time saves ten,"
- "Have we arrived yet?,"
- "The end is proximate,"
- "We hold these truths to be obvious,"
- "No 180-degree turn,"
- "Every Thomas, Richard, and Harold,"
- *"From Here to Forever,"*
- *"Greetings, Dolly!,"*
- *"The Red Letter,"*
- *"The Scarlet Badge of Courage,"*
- *"Orange Is the New Ebony,"* and
- "Cinch your seat belts."

If you laughed or even smiled at those poor substitutes, as you may have at, say, "roman o'clay," you did so at least in part because, like sveltes, the ways in which they are wrong have some relationship to their correct cousins. A cockeyed person is still eyed.

Among linguists there is a longstanding dispute about whether the metaphorical derivations of words linger in those words—whether what words mean now somehow contains and affects the meanings that preceded their carrying-over and their subsequent "burial" in the process of being transported. In the previous sentence, for example, does the Latin word for "tongue"—*lingua*—in any way "live" in "linguists," even if the writer/utterer of that word doesn't know the derivation? Does the basic, physical meaning of "stand" dwell somewhere within "longstanding"? Do the Greek origins of "metaphorical"—*meta* meaning "over" and *pherein* meaning "carry"—affect our use of the word in any way? Does the Latin word *derivare* —"to draw off water or a stream from its source"—flow in a significant way into "derivations"? Are we aware on any level, or does it matter on any level, that "linger" is perfectly related to the word "long"? Or, for that matter, that "perfectly" descends from the Latin words *per* and *facio*, meaning "done through"?

In his book *Philosophy in the Flesh,* George Lakoff—a cognitive linguist who has written influentially about language and politics and who has found himself embroiled in an ongoing argument with another, even more famous cognitive scientist/linguist, Steven Pinker—has written, "The mistake . . . [is] that those things in our cognition that are most alive and most active are those that are conscious. On the contrary, those that are most alive and most deeply entrenched, efficient, and powerful are those that are so automatic as to be unconscious and effortless."

On the other hand, in *The Oxford Companion to the*

English Language, Tom McArthur writes, "Many venerable metaphors have been literalized into everyday items of language: a clock has a *face* (unlike human or animal face), and on that face are *hands* (unlike biological hands)."

And in his article "More about Metaphor," Max Black is more emphatic on this matter: "[A] so-called dead metaphor is not a metaphor at all, but merely an expression that no longer has a pregnant metaphorical use." Like — I'm guessing Black would say — "fall in love," "foothills," "branches of medicine." But, then, what do we think of the word "pregnant" in that quotation? Is its metaphorical aspect alive within the word? I think so.

In this linguistic duel the next thrust comes from Zoltán Kövecses, in *Metaphor: A Practical Introduction*:

> The "dead metaphor" account misses an important point: namely, that what is deeply entrenched, hardly noticed, and thus effortlessly used is most active in our thought. The metaphors . . . may be highly conventional and effortlessly used, but this does not mean that they have lost their vigor in thought and that they are dead. On the contrary, they are "alive" in the most important sense — they govern our thought — they are "metaphors we live by."

Finally, in *The Body in Question*, Gregory Dawes parries with:

Because a term is used which was originally metaphorical, that is, which came from one domain of experience to define another, one cannot conclude that it necessarily continues to bring with it the associations which it had in that other domain. If it is a truly "dead" metaphor, it will not.

Well, maybe it is a kind of romanticism to believe that when you say "tomato" (or "tomahto"), the word contains its Nahuatl origin *tamatl,* which meant "swelling fruit." But it's not romantic at all to believe that choosing the right word—the word that in its present meaning *and* beginnings is helpful in getting across what you want to get across—will help to ratify what you are saying or writing. What we say and what we write will have more impact and influence and power if our words are well chosen, not only in their denotations, but also true to their connotations and parentages—true to, or at least consistent with, their histories.

Shakespeare, Sir Philip Sidney, Edmund Spenser, and Christopher Marlowe wrote at a time when the English language was coalescing out of, essentially, Anglo-Saxon (an outgrowth of North Germanic) and other linguistically blunt instruments, on the one hand, and, on the other, Latin. Those writers and many others, including, surely, ordinary people and their argots, all played a role in settling the language down a little from its earlier unruly rudiments. But they also were all neologizing terrors, expressing new ideas and concepts and distinctions by making up, stealing, and adapting words and phrases from other languages. For example, the National Geographic Society has estimated that from 1500 to 1660, Latin, Greek, and Romance languages added some thirty thousand new words to English.

Shakespeare above all, of course. According to some counts, he added two or three thousand new words to English, and hundreds of brilliant phrases that we now use as blithely as we open and close doors: "full circle," "sight for sore eyes," "break the ice," "for goodness' sake," and "foregone conclusion" among them.

Shakespeare's writings turned out to be sort of like stealth textbooks—or maybe "workbooks" would be more accurate—for the new English. Inventive and surprising as his plays and poems were, they paradoxically also served to *fix* the language. They helped to codify usages and grammar, in a loose-limbed way whose looseness we enjoy and employ to this day. ("It's me.") The tension between invention and regulation, and between Latin and Anglo-Saxon, is everywhere in his work, and if you think Shakespeare himself didn't understand that he was playing with brilliant and creative verbal fire, all you have to read is

> *Will all great Neptune's ocean wash this blood*
> *Clean from my hand? No; this my hand will rather*

The multitudinous seas incarnadine,
Making the green one red.
                    —*Macbeth*, Act 2, Scene 2

It's as if by invoking the Roman god Neptune, Shakespeare is signaling the approach of the fell footfalls of the Latinate polysyllabic monstrosity to follow the plain speech—"the multitudinous seas incarnadine." So much blood that its sea-tainting volume deserves a fancy description that you may not understand. And if you don't understand it, Shakespeare explains it in the next line—"making the green one red." The miniaturizing involved in "one" really gets me, as does the whole schoolmarmish tone of the simplified, monosyllabic paraphrase. It's as if Macbeth is taking time out from his despair to do a little explication of his own.

In that passage you can feel Shakespeare consciously mining the resources of the new language he was crucial in forming. He's having fun. He's showing off. He's also demonstrating the differing tones of this new, or at least refitted, instrument called English.

So: Is it to be "chew" or "masticate"? "Position" or "job"? "Boss" or "superior"? "Lie" or "prevaricate"? "Belly" or "abdomen"? "Die" or "expire"? Choosing between Latin-derived words and their Anglo-Saxon equivalents—and often within those two groups ("superior" or "manager," "belly" or "stomach")—can make an important, sometimes critical difference in the tenor, quality, and originality of what we're saying or writing.

This Latin/Anglo Saxon situation is the heart of the complexity and creativity of English. But there are other important parts of our linguistic anatomy besides the heart. Let's call Arabic a kidney: admiral, adobe, albatross, etc. American Indian languages a spleen: moccasin, moose, papoose, pecan. Japanese the other kidney: karaoke, tycoon, hibachi. Hindi and Urdu (some of the best-sounding words) a couple of ribs: cot, dinghy, cheetah, guru, juggle, thug. African languages a pancreas: banana, jumbo, zebra, yam. Norwegian a cerebellum: fjord, krill, ski, salmon. Tagalog an earlobe: manila, boondocks.

Immigrant words from foreign languages meet no barrier except usefulness and usage to gain entry into English — unlike human immigrants into English-speaking nations, who often meet resistance, if not hostility, everywhere they try to go. This Welcome Wagon for new words, in combination with the huge reserves of Anglo-Saxon and Latin/French words, helps to explain why English has a larger vocabulary than any other language. It's so large as to be fundamentally uncountable. It waxes and wanes every day, but mostly waxes. According to a number of sources, we have about one million words to get right or wrong.

But we don't by any means depend on other languages for additions to the family. Our flexible and improvisational way of speaking and writing our own language supplies us with a never-ending stream of neologisms. Many of these coinages, which often are struck by combinations, lose their currency after a few years. But many of them remain of the realm, thus expanding the treasury. "Chick lit," "staycation," "onesie," "cyberbully," "infotainment," "locavore," "guesstimate," etc. Those relative newcomers have a reasonable chance of sticking around. The Internet's lingo has not only added hundreds and hundreds of words to everyday speech, but social media, one of its products, have exponentially expanded the volume of written communication, thus allowing more people to fool around with our language, often distilling it into shorter forms (Twitter, most obviously).

The etymologies of English words not only help to explain and rationalize some of the funny mistakes we make with them (like "svelte," of course), but their infinitely creative origins, their spontaneous combustions, and the imperfections that inevitably accompany a world language adopted by non-native speakers multiply and enrich the opportunities for these kinds of mistakes. Honestly, I don't know if other languages are as error-fertile as ours. I doubt it.

Along the linguistics Internet trail, you will find comments like the following, by a blogger named "bardic," on a site called MetaFilter, a homey, general-interest community weblog with forty thousand members — which is, according to *Time,* which named the site among its Fifty Best, "remarkably free of trolls, griefers and other anonymous jerks."

English's strengths and weaknesses are inextricably linked—it's a mutt, a carpet-bag, and a sponge all at the same time . . . The only rule in English is that there will be multiple exceptions . . . Blame 1066 when the French took over a largely Germanic speaking nation called England and made their language the official one, as opposed to the native one . . . This led to the trainwreck that is modern English . . .

I'm currently studying Korean . . . The one thing I appreciate is that its alphabet (Hangul) makes the sounds that it's supposed to, always . . . The Korean college students I teach often complain that "Teacher, English is not fair!" And they're absolutely right.

English is a marvelous jumble, a mutational jungle of verbiflora and -fauna, bordering directly on the African svelte.

Deeper in a non-metaphorical jungle, you might find the most brilliant talker in all parrotdom—the African grey. If you capture one of these guys, and are callously indifferent to violating wild fauna's right to its place in nature, you might want to keep him in what an ad in the *Berkshire Record* called a

33. rod iron parrot cage.

WROUGHT IRON OFTEN *is* rod iron, and in fact the cage depicted was, as you might expect, made out of wrought-iron rods. This is heavy-metal svelte, phonetically almost perfect.

Today's "wrought" has been wrought from the past participle of the Middle English *werken*—"to work." And "wrought iron" first appeared in print in 1703. A few centuries ago, "overwrought" meant, simply, "overworked," as "wrought" was still the past participle of the transitive verb "work."

"Rod" has served many lexical purposes, from a means of punishment the sparing of which will spoil children; to cones' retinal business partner; to what seems to me a strangely arbitrary unit of measurement (15½ feet), more arbitrary than most others; to, slangily, penis and gun.

"Parrot," too, may—questionably—be distantly related to the word "penis," as some experts believe that it descends from "Pierre," French for "Peter." The original English term for this bird was "popinjay," which is derived from the Arabic *babagha*, allegedly onomatopoetic for the cry of this bird.

Though I must say that I once had a yellow-headed

amazon parrot (now an endangered species) who said nothing remotely like *babagha*. He—Edward J. Brownstein, MD, named after a psychoanalyst—said very little at all, in fact. I inadvertently taught him "What are you doing, Ed?" by saying it to him from time to time when I got home from the office. He would work it—as in, "What're yuh," "yuh doin' Ed," "are yuh doin'," etc.—and then cackle, exactly like the woman who cleaned my apartment, who found the mere existence of Ed hilarious. Ed also mastered "All news all the time," because I left WINS on the radio for him sometimes. And he exactly imitated the fire-engine sirens from a couple of blocks away, on Broadway.

His cage was not rod or wrought iron but just a pet-store golden-rod one. He was a good bird who made angry noises at any female who came near me. Guys were OK. He could have been a female, actually. It's hard to sex a parrot. S/he thought of my index finger as a twig and before his wings were clipped would fly around the room and land on it.

Sometimes, when Ed really got himself into squawking, the only way to make him stop was to put a cover over his cage. You could say that, like a train in a memoir sent to me at Random House, he

34. shuttered to a stop.

WHEN YOU THINK of a shutter, the chances are you don't think of the act of shutting anything—the way you might visualize the act of opening when you say "opener" —but of the physical object the word designates. Of course a shutter is indeed something that shuts or partially shuts something—a window's view—but the action is, well, shuttered within the word. The numerous and uniform slats on the kind of shutter that has slats are a physical analog of the act of shuddering—a series of numerous quick movements that are rapidly and at least somewhat uniformly repeated.

Quick movements that are rapidly and at least somewhat uniformly repeated bear a strong connection to a tweet that asked the question

35. If I masterbait in a plane, is it a hijacking?

NOW, HERE IS someone (a man, we will assume) who is clever enough to write or at least cite a pretty good-bad dirty joke but who is also orthographically challenged. In writing, as in standup, timing matters, and here the svelte sabotages the punch line.

"Masturbate" has its origins in Latin, in words that convey defilement and dishonor, and some etymologists say that it's related to "stupefaction" and "stupid." I can't do anything with "masterbait" but smile. Well, wait: "to master"—"to take control of" or "to be proficient at"—does have a certain relevance here, maybe. And so does "bait," in its temptational sense. These connotations may explain why those I've shown this svelte to have laughed extra-hard. Or maybe the altitudinous self-pleasuring pun of "hijacking," so fittingly svelted earlier, doesn't detract from but supplements the svelte that precedes it.

IN ANOTHER TWEET, a message, also on the sexual side, a guy tells some lucky girl,

36. Your dairy air looks rather ravishing from this vantage point.

IT'S POSSIBLE THAT "dairy air" is a Sirification, but this mistake is too good to miss. Few compliments about that part of the anatomy have achieved such inadvertent elegance, especially with the euphony of "ravishing" and "vantage."

"Dairy" is kind of perfect here, since it derives from the Old English *daege*, a female servant or maid, which is related to "dey," which is in turn related to "dough." Yes. And in French, *derrière* was originally an adverb, for "behind, from the back," so its anatomical application in English is a euphemism, and a kind of joke, taking an abstract piece of language and making it physical.

As with other body parts and actions involving basic functions, our fundaments have generated a host of substitutes, almost all of them (like "fundament") humorous in original intent: "moon," "caboose," "duff," "moneymaker," "keister," "booty," five or six variants of the Yiddish word *tuchus*, "fanny," and "business class."

Maybe the "dairy air" tweeter was a nudist who, if he ever met the dairy air's owner, would say to her (as yet another tweeter wrote),

37. Please bare with me.

THIS IS A pretty common misspelling, like "accomo-date" for "accommodate," "untill" for "until," "wierd" for "weird," "lollypop" for "lollipop," and so on. These mistakes are approaching in frequency the kind that have, in the past, become so common as to achieve acceptibility. Acceptability. Through analyzing usage data, the *Oxford English Dictionary* tries to keep track of this phenomenon, and when the "incorrect"—they don't use "correct" or "incorrect," but I do—spelling begins to rival or overtakes the correct one, the *OED* includes the former mistake as a "valid alternative" to the original spelling of the word. Some examples of the kinds of statistics the dictionary takes into consideration when deciding on "valid alter-natives": For every 97 times "moot point" appears, "mute point" appears 3. "Sleight of hand" to "slight of hand," 85 to 15. "Toe the line" to "tow the line," 84 to 16. "Fazed by" to "phased by," 71 to 29. "Free rein" to "free reign," 54 to 46. And all the way to "strait-laced" giving way to "straight-laced," 34 to 66.

So, then, the straight-laced *OED* has pronounced "straight-laced" a valid alternative to "strait-laced."

I wonder if this latitudinarianism would extend to the frequent, sensible svelte

98

38. Straight of Hormuz.

THE KINSHIP BETWEEN "strait" and "straight" is almost a twinship, though their backgrounds are, surprisingly, quite different. "Strait" comes from the Old French *estrait*, for "a pass, a defile." Like "Straight of Hormuz," "strait and narrow" would be a successful play on words because it makes use of the words' similar meanings. So would, at least sort of: "He went strait," "Get strait to the point," "Let's get this strait," and "strait arrow." (Actually, check that: "Strait and narrow" turns out not to be some new, sveltish invention of mine or any other contemporary's, because the phrase was used as far back as the fourteenth century.)

"Straight" comes from the Old English *streccan*, "to stretch," I suppose because when you stretch something, like a lump of dough, it generally becomes straighter.

When you find yourself in the "Straight of Hormuz" these days, considering the conflicts surrounding that body of water, you may find yourself waiting with

39. baited breath

This one may be on the *OED* "valid alternative" list now, but I still think it's a svelte, one that works because of the connotation of suspense it shares with "bated breath." If you're fishing and there's a big one swimming around the bait on your hook, you may hold—abate—your breath in instinctive game-hunting silence.

As far as we know, "bated breath" first showed up in writing in *King Lear*. The phrase also appears to be the only such usage of the word "bated" in this adjectival sense. We don't have "bated appetite," "bated interest," etc., as idioms.

In order to make sounds, our breath has to traverse what *The New Yorker,* of all places, a year or so ago referred to as our

40. vocal chords.

THIS SUBSTITUTION EXPLAINS its own logic, but what it doesn't tell you is that in their backgrounds "cord" and "chord" are closely related, the latter being a variation of the former that took on its own separate meaning. A "chord"—"related notes in music"—first appeared in the late-sixteenth century and was probably a shortening of "accord." From the Latin *chorda,* for "catgut" or "string" of a musical instrument. The "h" crept back into the word in around 1600, apparently in part to distinguish it from "cord." Very tangled, and so let's get out of here and go to the other end of the human body, where we can

41. tow the line.

ANOTHER COMMON SVELTE, this one earns its place here because the meaning of the misspelling fits so well with its correct spelling. Both "tow the line" and "toe the line" have pedal overtones—undertones—and evocations of duty and discipline. In fact, "tow" comes down to us from a Proto-Indo-European ancestor, *deuk-*, meaning "to pull" or "to draw," and by extension "to lead."

Many sources say that "toe the line" comes from the British "toe the mark," which started on board ships: The captain would draw a line on the deck and order the crew to assemble along that line. I have no idea why. For inspection, maybe. Many sources cite other lineages—taking attendance at British schools, lining up for footraces, what opponents once had to do in boxing matches before the fight began.

Each of these last three, more frequent spelling errors (like what's coming next, which once again is pedal in nature) was a

42. shoe-in

FOR INCLUSION IN THIS BOOK, because like "shoe-in" itself, they fit easily into the sveltique meaningful-mistake category. The correct first syllable, "shoo," is in some conflict with "in," since it's a cry usually meant to drive or scare something away ("Shoo, fly!").

When you read "shoe-in," you almost automatically conflate the meaning of the real phrase with putting your foot into a comfortable, accommodating shoe. Right? And no wonder, from a historical point of view. Because the expression "shoo-in" may have started with horseracing, indicating "easy winner" or even "fixed winner," and horses have special shoes—another subconscious association that makes the svelte look right. Some commentators have speculated that the "shoo" part of "shoo-in" is an "instinctive" word for movement away from or toward a location; it has equivalents in other languages—for instance, *schu,* in German. And "in"—well, think of "in-crowd," "in like Flynn," etc. That is, something to do with success.

The subject of horses brings back to mind the *OED* blog that analyzes and lists wrongs that become something like right. One of the most outlandish and wonderful examples of a verbal wrong becoming right is the phrase "curry favor." Here's the story: The original version of this phrase was "curry Favel," referring to a horse in the fourteenth-century French allegorical poem *"Roman de Fauvel."* Fauvel, the horse, was renowned for his equine cunning and deceptions, so to "curry Favel" meant to "stroke" or "groom" him—metaphorically, to act in a hypocritically deceitful way.

So "curry favor" started its career as a svelte. You can easily understand why the wrong became right when you think of the servile, figuratively obsequious note in the word "curry." (You might think that curry powder shares its background with the verb "curry." It doesn't—it's derived from the Tamil *kari*, which is a sauce or relish for rice. You might even say you sort of curry plain dishes with curry.)

I wonder if, like a horse in another source-lost svelte, sent to me by a friend, Favel ever

43. started to cantor.

LIKE "CANTOR," the leader of song and chant (a related word) in Judaism and many Christian faiths, "canter" sounds a religious note. It comes from "the Canterbury gallop," the easy pace at which pilgrims on the way to Canterbury rode. It's a nice coincidence, in the Canterbury connection, that the comedian/actor/singer/vaudevillian Eddie Cantor co-wrote the song "Merrily We Roll Along."

Music also plays a more defensibly historical part in the name "Canterbury," since in the eighteenth century, the archbishop of that place, Frederick Cornwallis, commissioned a piece of furniture, a music stand, to go with the piano, which was beginning its ascendancy as the domestic keyboard instrument of choice. That music stand, and also, confusingly, a decorative piece for storing or displaying papers and magazines, were, and are, called Canterburies.

How does it feel, I wonder, to have a piece of furniture named after you? The Pembroke table, the Sutherland table, the Wellington chest. The Queen Anne stuff. The Murphy bed.

Over here, in our antique-furniture section, and while we're talking about furniture named for people, we have what a Facebook friend of mine said that a seriously orthographically challenged Facebook friend of hers referred to as

44. a mirrow and a chester drawers.

IF NOT "MIWOW," "mirrow" is the standard child's effort at pronouncing "mirror," with all its confusing and
enunciation-defying "r"s. Or did she mean a Miró? A
"chester drawers" has more packed inside it. "Chester"
is derived from the Latin *castrum*, "fortified place," and is
related to "castle." "Chest" comes from the Proto-Indo-
European *kiste*, for "woven container." In the sixteenth
century, "chest" replaced "breast" as the gender-neutral
noun for that part of the body, though you still hear
"breast" used that way from time to time. ("Hope springs
eternal . . .") I remember being adolescently embarrassed
when my mother-in-law, during a poker game, said to
me, "Breast your cards!"

So furniture chests and human chests are both con-
tainers, and in a sense they are both fortifications, pro-
tected places—chesters: a word that in itself and in its
variants, as found in Alcester, Lancaster, Cirencester,
Gloucester (pronounced Gloster), Leicester (pronounced
Lester), Tadcaster, Wroxeter, and Towcester, supplies the
last two syllables for so many localities in England and
America.

And, OK, mirrows often accompany chester drawerses. In Latin, *mirare* means "to look at" and is a variant of *mirari*, "to wonder at, admire." The word "miracle" proceeds from that meaning. Drawers are what you draw from the chesters, and to draw with a pencil is to pull the pencil along the paper. That meaning started somewhere around 1200, and a little later people started drawing their weapons. It all goes back to the PIE word for "drag."

Across the Channel from all the British chesters and Canterburies, in Aix-en-Provence, you can stop for lunch at the Burger Bar, which proudly calls itself

45. Le Maison du HandBurger.

IN GERMAN, *burg* originally meant a high, fortified place, the *Deutsch* equivalent to "chester's" derivation from the Latin *castrum*, a fortified encampment. There has always been tension and competition — and too often war — between the French and the Germans, so maybe the Burger Bar doesn't want to acknowledge that this dish got its name from Hamburg, Germany, as frankfurter got its name from Frankfurt (and "wiener" from Vienna). If the Burger Bar served frankfurters, it might call them francfurters. Instead, the eatery appropriated the old-fashioned way of making burgers — by hand — and so HanDBurger sort of makes verbal sense.

There is often some peril involved in crossing not only the English Channel but all bodies of water, a peril especially if, as a friend of mine described himself in an email, you are

46. stuck in the styx.

BAD ENOUGH TO have to cross this terminal river to reach the Underworld, but to be *stuck* in it, especially since the name comes from the Greek for "the hateful," seems like an afterlife of slow torture, particularly for city dwellers, who so dislike both delays and suburbs.

If my correspondent had written it correctly, "stuck in the sticks," which has become common parlance for this predicament, it would contain not only the same kind of alliterative poetry but also a kind of verbal play, as "stuck" is the past tense of "stick." But "sticks," as a slang term for the suburbs and beyond, almost certainly comes from pejoratively diminutivizing all those trees. By combining the elements of stasis, death, and hellishness, this svelte sums up the punishment that many suburbanites feel they suffer in living where they live.

To hear the lamentations of those shades wandering around Hades forever must be—as a college fundraiser wrote of some affecting alumni stories—

47. heart-rendering.

"RENDER" AND "REND" have been first cousins for many centuries, and the word "rent" may well be a second cousin, or even a first cousin once removed. We'll get to that. But first, "to render" means not only "to draw out the fat from meat," but also, by a considerable metaphorical stretch, "to offer a version of a song" or "to create a visual image or sculpture or some other representation of an object, scene, or person." And also "to pay or give up or convey to," as when Jesus instructed his followers to render unto Caesar the things that were Caesar's, but only demonstrably Caesar's, the rest being reserved for the Deity.

All these renderings—even the fat rendering—have in common the concept of taking and/or transferring. Heat the fat from the meat. Render it. Listen to John Coltrane's rendition of "My Favorite Things." We've already accounted for the idea of paying up, the discharging of obligations, with Jesus and Caesar.

So maybe someday the medicos will come up with a procedure that renders the cholesterol and other cardiological fatty deposits from the body. They might call it "cardiac lipid reduction," but I will call it "heart rendering."

As for "rend," well, its etymological background has much to do with taking—as in tearing something apart or, more strictly, tearing one thing from another, a kind of violent rendering. The Bible, violent as it is, rends and rends all over the place:

> Say unto them which daub it with untempered morter, that it shall fall: there shall be an overflowing shower; and ye, O great hailstones, shall fall; and a stormy wind shall rend it.

> And there was an hole in the midst of the robe, as the hole of an habergeon, with a band round about the hole, that it should not rend.

> Howbeit I will not rend away all the kingdom; but will give one tribe to thy son for David my servant's sake, and for Jerusalem's sake which I have chosen.

English has rent "rend" from the German *Rinde*, for "crust" or "bark"—both of which, like the English "rind" that the German word gave rise to, are often torn away. And now, finally, we come to the other "rent," which has been torn from the Latin *rendere*, also obviously the source of "render." If you haven't experienced "rent"—for, say, a house, apartment, or car—as a kind of tearing away (of money), you're lucky and probably rich. The etymology of the word includes or at least involves the etymologies of "render" and "rend."

Modern international military conflicts have presented us with a new and ugly meaning for "rendition." It has always denoted the act of transferring a prisoner from one jurisdiction to another, usually to the place where the crime was committed, as in from one state to another. But these days it refers to the relocation of suspects, especially terrorism suspects, to a place, a country, where the laws or the authorities do not concern themselves about torture.

But back to the sveltes. I don't want to ignore

48. morter—

FROM EZEKIEL 13:10, as rendered in the previous svelte: "Say unto them which daub it with untempered morter..."

This is either a typo or a genuine svelte for "mortar." But in the Ivy League slang of the 1950s, "to mort" meant "to die," and a "morter" was someone in the process of dying or someone who has just completed that process. And "mort" now, however aristocratically, refers to the note sounded by a hunting horn at the death of the quarry.

"Mortar" works hard. It's a bowl used for crushing (by means of its brother, the pestle); it's the substance that secures one brick to another; and it's a kind of artillery piece, a gun, like a container, that receives a shell, essentially a bomb, which is fired at a steep angle and therefore falls at a steep, detonating angle. It is a bomb fired from the ground. And, with "board," it's the square, flat, hand-held platform on which bricklayers put their mortar and from which they trowel it up and apply it. The academic adoption of "mortar board" —the flat thing on top of a graduate's yarmulkesque cap—is lovely, marrying, as it does, the manual and the mental.

How could anyone confuse a military conflict with an act of begging or pleading? Easy. Just write a letter to the Trinidad *Guardian* and say,

49. I besiege you to employ the services of two special agents from the Federal Bureau of Investigation.

MAYBE THE WRITER sent this same letter every day for a month, turning his beseeching into a besieging. In any case, this error's appropriateness speaks for itself.

"Siege" goes back, a little circuitously, to the Latin *sedere*, "to sit." Starting in the thirteenth century, in what was to become English, "siege" meant "seat," as in the "Siege Perilous"—the seat at King Arthur's Round Table that only the knight who would end up finding the Holy Grail could occupy. And there is, amazingly, someone so dumb that, up until the very minute of this writing, he never quite got why the seat was perilous. It should be the Siege Marvelous, or the Siege Supreme, or something like that, he is said to have reasoned. This failure to put one and one together—to understand that it was perilous because if the wrong knight sat there, he would die—is embarrassing to that person, I have it on good authority. I guess he was just looking on the sunny side.

The modern use of "siege," for a kind of stationary attack outside an enemy stronghold, developed because the besieging forces more or less sat down, or settled down, outside their target.

It seems that three knights who tried to sit in the Siege Perilous were burned to a crisp. According to another ancient text, some pretenders were "swallowed up." The question arises: How did Galahad know it was safe for him to sit down in the S.P.? Thomas Malory, in *Le Morte d'Arthur*, says that "a very old knight" led Galahad and bade him sit down. But why on earth would Galahad have trusted some very old knight? He might have been dotty, for God's sake. But it all worked out.

More or less as "besiege" did with "siege," "beseech" grew from an earlier root, which meant "seek." In this case, the "be-" prefix serves as an intensifier rather than a verbifier.

At my high school, during a Tack Attack that went viral for a while, every chair was a Siege Perilous. In Spanish One, I sat down and did not burn to a crisp and was not swallowed up, but I did rise very quickly, and in pain. A kid sitting next to me—younger and smaller, so there was no dignified way to retaliate—was laughing his own ass off.

At least this wound to my dignity didn't result in what an online forum referred to as a (get ready for disgusting)

50. pus jewel.

MAYBE BEST NOT to go into the background of "pus" or "pustule," as it features stinking, rotting, swelling, decaying, and so on. Some authorities believe that the word "pus" may have developed from a simple, nonverbal exclamation of disgust. "Jewel" is more pleasant and more complicated. Some etymologists have linked it to "joke" and "joy." So this svelte cleverly marries two opposite effects and in the process conjures up a gross but in some ways accurate visual image. Sorry.

Here's to forgetting all about this entry by listening to a more pleasantly infectious song by a group identified in a record producer's diary as

51. the Red Hot Chile Peppers.

DO YOU REMEMBER the "Aztechs," with their Nahuatl language? Or are you just skimming? "Chile" is probably a Nahuatl or other native word for the land and may—in a pretty coincidence, given our word "chilly"—have meant something like "cold" or "winter." "Chili" is definitely from Nahuatl and refers to the eponymous peppers. These two words and their spellings have tangled with each other so often that "Chile peppers" and "chile peppers" are threatening to become certified as acceptable substitutes by a number of sources.

Though the *OED* doesn't appear to see it that way. What it does like is to list rhyming words, usefully enough for doggerelists, I suppose. In this case it's

Billie, billy, Dili, dilly, filly, frilly, ghillie, gillie, Gilly, hilly, Lillee, lily, Lyly, papillae, Philly, Piccadilly, piccalilli, silly, skilly, stilly, Tilly, willy-nilly.

(Loving "papillae" over here.)
Personally, I can do without chili but would be devastated to find that I was

52. lack-toes intolerant,

AS AN EMAIL to me from a writer put it—seriously, I think. "Lactose intolerance" has, unfortunately, given rise to some deliberate, lame (sorry!) puns: lack toes and tolerant, lack toast 'n' tolerant. I don't know of a single person who is a toe-ist—intolerant of those untoed. But a lot of women (and some of their men) like toeless stockings and other such garments. "Toeless" in this sense is a paradox: The garments lack toes, thus making the actual toes all the more prominent.

"Lactose" and "intolerant" are, developmentally speaking, boring words. But "toes"—now we're talking. "Toe" may have started its orthographically elaborate journey as the Proto-Indo-European *deik*—"to show." Many PIE words use the same noun for our toes and fingers. And from this origin we get "diction." And "digit," through the Latin *digitus*, "finger" or "toe." There are ten of each of those things, unless we are lack-toes, and so a digit is any numeral from one to ten. Once again: "Viola!"

Some people have an extra toe or finger, or extra toes or extra fingers or extra toes *and* extra fingers. The condition is called polydactylism. You could say they have a

53. pluthora

OF DIGITS. I came across "pluthora" in a real-estate ad. The house for sale had a "pluthora of amenities." Simple typo? Apparently not. Further research revealed a plethora of this svelte. A plethora of pluthoras. The mistake may soon turn into what the *OED* calls a "valid alternative," no doubt upsetting a pluthora of scholars.

This is a perfect svelte, maybe not pronunciationally but definitely meaning-wise. "Plethora" means "abundance," and sometimes "overabundance," and comes from the Greek *plethein*—"to be full." The Latin word *plus*, meaning "more," goes back to a Proto-Indo-European root meaning "full." And so it makes sense: A pluthora must be an overoverabundance.

How do some people with polydactylism deal with the extras? They or their parents have them surgically removed. On the other, er, hand, a cooking column asks,

54. How do you remove oil from chettar cheese?

NO ONE KNOWS. Because there's no such thing as chettar cheese. But *chettar* is the Pali word for "cutter" or "destroyer," so chettar cheese might be an extremely sharp cheddar cheese. And no, "chettar" isn't English, but it's a handsome little mistake, so back off. But not so far as to hazard sailing into what a university press release called

55. unchartered waters.

AS YOU MIGHT EXPECT, "chart" and "charter" carry the same Latin genes, but their meanings, although now different, are related in specific ways. Un*charted* waters are almost necessarily waters that are un*chartered*—without a treaty to govern them. Lawless. "Uncharted waters" has come to be an idiom, some might say a cliché, for situations that are unfamiliar, dangerous, filled with risk, at least partly because pirates could ply such real-world seas —especially if they were also unchartered—with little fear of capture and punishment.

A blog post warning that climbing a certain cliff was not for

56. the feint of heart

MIGHT SAY THE SAME of sailing unchartered waters.

Feint, in Old French, meant "weak" or "lazy," so in its background this svelte works in the usual amphibious —I mean, ambiguous—way. And "faint" and "feint," and "feign" and even "fain," have crossed paths historically for centuries. A feint—to the left, say, if you're a running back in football—is a movement cut short in order to fool a pursuer. So you could say it's not only a deceptive action but an incomplete or unrealized one. You are *feigning* an action, and so also, in a way, it's "faint."

"Fain" played a part in my folkie upbringing, since I heard Ewan MacColl sing the Child ballad "Lord Randall" when I was about eight. His Scottish burr rendered "make my bed soon, for I'm weary with hunting, and I fain would lie down" as "mak my bed soon, for I'm weary wi' huntin', and I fain would lie doon." This seemed to me a much more interesting way to speak English than the way I and everyone around me spoke it, and I affected my pathetic version of a Scottish accent for some months, saying, when I was tired, "I fain would lee doon." (I improvised "lee.")

"Fain" and "feign" and "faint" are rattling around here

together for a genuinely svelte-related reason—as an introduction to an obsessive but occasionally hilarious website, verbotomy.com, where visitors coin new words to express new and highly differentiated concepts. (For example, if you're "shrimpatico," you have sympathy and affection for lower life forms. If what you're eating contains harmful chemicals, call them "badditives.") There, they have married "feign" and "faint" and come up with "feignt," which means "to be physically overcome by a sudden illness or disability when asked to participate in unrewarding activities—like work, or household chores."

Almost every topic has a website, or many websites, devoted to it now. And as a rule they

57. oparate without interfearance

— AND ALSO, as in that very quote from a fantasy and science fiction online forum, without copy-editing oversight ("oversite" might be better). "Oparate" is a simple spelling error and doesn't yield much in the way of history. "Operate," on the other hand, does include the word "opera," which started out as a plural noun for the Latin "opus." The early vocal performances that led to what we think of as operas consisted of separate vocal works, each one an opus and all together, therefore, *opera*— "works."

"Interfearance" makes instinctive sense as a verbal mistake—a frightening occurrence that gets in the way. Fear by itself usually presents an interference with a baseline state of calm or routine. This makes the name of the British club band called Interfearence something of a puzzle, since its music is standard and often purposely repetitive four-on-the-floor semi-electronica. Sorta dull, unless you've taken a big drug or drunk something very helpful. The names of Interfearence's tracks faintly echo, sveltically, its name: "Xtradition," "TheUnder," "Prosecutioner." Here's how they describe themselves:

Interfearence are a London based outfit who make original club tunes that offer a refreshingly twisted alternative to traditional 4-on-the-floor house. Their sophomore album . . . is packed with tracks that jump inside your mind with an instant mood, an infectious bassline, driving percussion, and trippy vocal hooks. Their unique formula references the heady days of clubbing when the Stone Roses might get played alongside 808 State, where influences are truly eclectic—a mix of psychedelia, exotic drumming, moody soundscapes, and a whole chunk of dirty digital funk.

Ah, yes, he says—Stone Roses and 808 State. For all he knows, those were indeed the headiest of dirty-digital-funk days.

I want you to know that I managed to

58. levy those words with a smile,

RUEFUL THOUGH THE SMILE may have been, for, dating me, the only "Stone" groups I really know are Linda Ronstadt's Stone Poneys, the Rolling Ones, and Sly and the Family. Though now that I've listened to Interfearence a little, I have to take back what I just said, because their tracks are not only insanely danceable but musically witty. They *leaven* their basic four-on-the-floor dance music with Chipmunks-style drone vocals, ethereal girl refrains, and funny rap lyrics. Their rhyming is infectious.

"Levy" and "leaven" both involve "raise" but in different ways. "Levy," in reference to, say, taxes, means "raise" or "collect." Bakers use leavening to make bread rise. And "leaven" comes from the Latin *levare*, "to raise." And— wait, wait! "Levy" turns out to have exactly the same raising. It dates back to *levare* as well. This discovery just now makes me want to take a

59. bough,

AS JAYSON STARK once spelled "bow" in a column for espn.com, though the context was not taking a bow but a shot across one. "Bow" (both pronunciations) and "bough" are, like many sveltes, close etymological kin, both connoting grace, both invoking human anatomy— shoulders, particularly. You can feel the kinetic/aesthetic connection among a violin's graceful bow, an archer's bow, a deferential bow, a ship's handsome bow.

Bows for stringed instruments are often referred to as "fiddlesticks"; how that word—and "fiddle-de-dee" and "fiddle-faddle"—came to express skepticism or dismissal remains close to a mystery. But not quite a mystery, because the word "fiddle"—which, probably and improbably, is a remote derivation of "violin," believe it or not —has come to describe aimless or random hand motion. If you watch a violinist play, and blank out the music, his bow hand will look as though it's fiddling, in a manner visually opposite the artful music it's actually making.

To fiddle, with a violin or otherwise, your hand needs to have a

60. poseable thumb,

SOMETIMES WRITTEN AS "posable thumb," as employed on a circumcision website. Don't get snippy about this; it's a real svelte and a genuine source. A gentleman, possibly a gentile man, named Kenny tells us that circumcision cannot be "what seperates [*sic*] us from the animals either, we have a poseable thumb, we walk upright, we live in groups of others who we don't know, we have a currency system and a society."

"Poseable thumb," for "opposable thumb," possesses the usual svelte fittingness, for what is an opposable thumb if not posable? That is, unlike most mammals, we can "pose" our thumbs against our other fingers. "To pose" means either "to assume a still position," as for a painting or a photo shoot, or, by extension, "to impersonate or "to fake an identity." "Pose" derives from the Latin *pausare*—"to halt, cease, or rest." Thus, also, "pause."

Your hand also needs to have an opposable thumb to fully qualify as a hand—that is, in order to

61. pass mustard.

THIS SVELTE HAS numerous sources, including *The Motley Fool*, the name of an investment advisory newsletter. The newsletter may have been joking in its svelting, but many of the other sources clearly weren't.

There appears to be no etymological connection between "muster" and "mustard." The former comes down to us from the Latin *monstrare*, "to show." The English word "mustard" comes from the Anglo-Norman *mustarde* and Old French *mostarde*. The first syllable derives from the Latin *mustum* ("must" means "young wine"), and the second originated with the Latin *ardens*—"hot," "flaming." The condiment was originally prepared by making the ground seeds of the mustard plant into a paste with must. Despite the historical distance between the two words, I suggest here that "cut the mustard" bears a striking connection to "pass muster."

But if you dig around, as I have maniacally done, you will find that "cut the mustard" may well have a more interesting background than many of the other words and phrases anatomized here. In the nineteenth century in America, if a railroad wanted to build tracks across a farmer's land, the company had to see to it that the mustard weed that tended to grow along those tracks, spreading vigorously and threatening crops, was kept in check — cut down. The phrase "cut the mustard" came to mean "perform a service or function or obligation well, properly."

It's not surprising, then, that "cut the mustard" came to have a sexual overtone, especially about men, as in the Ernest Tubb song "Too Old to Cut the Mustard," whose last verse implies that the girls no longer line up for the singer's favors.

Researching derivations and original sources and discussions of the denotations and connotations of words and phrases can set up what an email to me described as a kind of lexical

62. cacoughany of sounds

IN YOUR BRAINPAN. "Cough" is in its essence onomatopoetic, as it is, with minor variations, in all the languages I inspected for their tussive terminology. Since a lot of coughing could easily—and often does, during musical performances—create a cacophony, a svelte once again earns its suitability stripes.

The first part of the word "cacophony" comes from the Ancient Greek *kakos*, "bad" or "unpleasant," and the second part from *phonos*, which, duh-ly, means "sound." And yes, as you might have expected and even hoped, it's possible, given *kakos*, that "caca" has a place in No. 62 here.

"Onomatopoeia," whose spelling earns me a red underline or an autocorrect nearly every time I try to type it, means the making of a word from a sound. Unlike the foreign relatives of "cough," it presents itself in the most wonderfully inconsistent way in efforts of different languages to make animal noises into words. Take a dog's bark as one example. In Russian, it's *gav*. Gav? Yes. In Romanian it's *ham*. Ham? Indonesian, *guk*. Turkish, *hev*. Korean, *meong*. My own dog, even though he's a Tibetan terrier, barks in English with a New York accent.

Lions say *murr* in Finnish.

None of these creatures should follow a Facebook post and take these comments about their cross-linguistic inconsistencies

63. ad homonym,

SINCE (a) the correct spelling is *ad hominem*, and these animals are quite specifically not human, and (b) the various sounds they make, according to their fellow country-animal humans, are precisely *not* homonymic—bafflingly do *not* sound alike.

I was going to tackle "homophone" vs. "homonym" vs. "homograph," but it's kind of a mess in there. "Homograph" applies to words that are written—thus the "graph"—exactly the same: "lead" and "lead," for example. "Homophone" refers to a word that is pronounced like another but has a different spelling and meaning: "to," "too," "two." "Homonym"—this is where I bog down, as the word has two different meanings, and one seems to be "homograph" and the other "homophone." We could call it a duonym or a binym. You can see why one might get a little lost here.

So "bee" and "be" are homosomethingorothers, and they find themselves cross-pollinated in a non-contexted svelte that a cousin sent to me—

64. wanna-bees.

MOST SOURCES AGREE that the noun "wanna-be" (or "wannabe") originated during the 1960s in surfer slang, to refer to those who wanted to be surfers but weren't, or those who were but were not very good at it. Since "bee" can mean a social gathering (sewing bee, for example, or quilting bee) or a competition (spelling bee), you can see the wannabe surfers feeling admiringly jealous as they watch the experts hang ten.

Because of their swarming habits and Aesopian fabledness, bees have landed in a lot of places in our language —annoying us in our bonnets, identifying simple laborers, designating industriousness, indicating patellar specialness, defining female royalty, teaming up with birds to summarize sex, in combination with wax to indicate something that is none of your business, and following a straight and quick path.

And when you drop the second "e"? The background of the word "be" is formidably complex. This etymological complexity, which the *OED* calls a "tangle," no doubt explains why it is the most irregular verb in our language, taking fourteen different forms for fourteen different grammatical functions—"be," "am," "are," "is," "was," "were," "being," "been." It also explains why we're going to move right along.

You will find wannabes in every sport, profession, and art. Henri Cole is no wannabe—he is a very good poet, and a generous one, who not long ago tweeted about seeing fellow poet Langston Hughes's name prominently displayed:

65. It cheers me to find a poet's name in lights on a marquis!

THIS SVELTE MADE me picture someone dressed up like the Marquis de Lafayette striding around Times Square with some kind of modern technological device that lit up his chest with LANGSTON HUGHES blinking on and off. It would cheer anyone, I think, but given the surreal nature of Times Square these days, an intermittently lit-up marquis might not be all that surprising.

"Marquis" originally designated the ruler of a border area, which was and sometimes still is, however archaically, referred to as a "march." "Marquee" comes from the French *marquise,* which designated a large canopy spread over a military officer's tent in order to distinguish it from the tents of the rank and file. As you might guess, these two words were probably once involved with each other, and they make a good svelte, as both contain the idea of prominence.

Speaking of the French language and the French military, a leader always hopes his troops will have what a publishing proposal for a nonfiction book called

66. esprit décor.

IF YOU BET that at least one home-furnishings establishment has adopted this as its name, you'd win. It's in Chesapeake, Virginia. *Esprit Décor* is also the name of a Canadian military magazine (which has nothing to do with interior design), the title of a recording by a rock group called the Wild Beasts, and a movie made in the Philippines. And, if you stretch just a little, you may be able to glimpse the fact that "esprit de corps," French for "group spirit and energy," has some very slim Venn-type relationship with "décor"—something to do with presentation and compatibility, or coordination.

"Esprit" on its own probably generated "spree," a derivation that speaks for itself. "Corps" in French means "body," and by extension a group of soldiers who fight together as one. Another descendant of this originally Latin family, "corpse," notably lacks esprit. It has given up the ghost—a spirit.

"Spirit" almost surely, and lyrically, comes from the Latin *spirare*, "to breathe." You begin, then, to see the anatomical/respirational poetry of "esprit de corps"—the breathing, the body. And you can also see why I consider this the perfect spot to take a second breather—another

147

BRAKE.

THE *OXFORD ENGLISH DICTIONARY* and the *OED Online* are, in the face of scholarly fragmentation, bravely clinging to their preeminent lexical authority in our language. Meticulous in its scholarship, resistant to judgments about correctness and incorrectness, humanistic yet objective in its outlook, distinguished in its history, creative in its adaptation to the Internet, and often funny, the *OED* again and again manages to show by implication that the origins, meanings, connotations, and pronunciations of words are consequential.

Another *OED*—the *Online Etymology Dictionary*—comes at its subject with similar rigor and humor, but with a more personal and sometimes eccentric touch, by its founder, Douglas Harper, who says of himself:

Harper is a graduate of Dickinson College, Carlisle, Pa., with a degree in history and English. He has been featured in a BBC production on the Welsh settlements in America, and has been interviewed as a source for historical articles by the Philadelphia Inquirer, Washington Post and many magazines. He was arguably the second-most-famous assistant city editor ever to work at the West Chester, Pa., "Daily Local News." The other was Dave Barry. The newspaper was affectionately known by its readers as the "Daily Lack of News."

Then there is the Eggcorn Forum, cited in the Introduction. I collected these sveltes myself, with the help of the similarly Introduction-cited James Gleick, but I have to admit that I sometimes looked to the Eggcorn Forum for backup and even for "collecting" an entry or maybe two. Its mistakes are sourced and receive knowledgeable and funny comments, and, like a hugely prudent and manic squirrel, it has, as of this writing, collected 643 eggcorns. More than a few of the sveltes taken in the wild here turn out also to appear on the list of eggcorns on the forum, but I did almost all of my own foraging.

The Language Log has proven to be another rich research source. Of its founding, it says:

Language Log was started in the summer of 2003 by Mark Liberman and Geoffrey Pullum. For nearly five years, it ran on the same *elderly linux box,* with the same 2003-era blogging software, sitting in a dusty corner of a group office at the Institute for Research in Cognitive Science at the University of Pennsylvania.

A number of other online and print sources added their own scholarship and commentary and sometimes jaunty opinions to the work of this book, among them english stackexchange.com, wordorigins.org, and alphadiction ary.com. But if you think this is all just a way of squeezing an Acknowledgments section into the main part of the book, think again. Because (a) it's actually about to turn into a Point, and (b) there's a real, somewhat redundant Acknowledgments thing at the end of the book.

The Point (but you still need to be patient): As of this writing, there are 1,300,000 links when you enter "barbecue websites" in the Google search bar. There are 16,600,000 for "hammocks." 30,300,000 for "drones for sale." 50,300,000 for "vanilla ice cream." 583,000 for "stalagmites." 676,000 for "stalactites," including 163,000 for "stalactite sales." 11,000,000 for "the Atlantic shelf." 9,230,000 for "shelf paper." 106,000,000 for "paper shelf." 442,000,000 for "Croatia." 67,100 for "Croatia mushrooms." 85,400 for "edible Serbian mushrooms." 325,000 for "poisonous Serbian mushrooms." 1,030,000 for "decorative mushrooms." 43,800 for "decorative mushroom *spores*." (Italics mine—couldn't resist.) 3,280 for "decorative mushroom stores." 1,010,000 for "Jonathan Franzen." 107,000 for "Johnny Frantzen." 147,000 for yours truly. 23,400,000 for "yours truly." 596,000,000 for "random search." 253,000,000 for "random Google search." 244,000 for "random froogle search." 427,000 for "random dribble." 417,000 for "random drivel." 457,000,000 for "hello, how are you?" 665,000 for "jes' fine." 120,000,000 for "just awful." 361,000,000 for "stop reading this list now." 262,000,000 for "stop writing this list now." 0 for "mordomity calicity."

So if I type a made-up random svelte into the Google search bar—well, here goes. I'll tell you what happens in a minute or two. I'll start with "perryodontics." OK, OK —no luck. Let's try "in a hartbeat." And there it is, on a Polish site, tekstowo.pl/. Another: "cholesteroil." Easy:

www.caloriecount.com › Forums › Foods
Jan 20, 2008—The Land of Lakes butter with canola oil and 60% reduced cholesteroil is surprisingly good. My 3-yr old butter junky is reaching for that instead.

The point: The Internet is to English (and other languages and all information, for that matter) as Vishnu is to the world: creator and destroyer. It is in the process of destroying old rules and creating new ones, as you can see from the *OED* site, which lists "misspellings" when they begin to challenge former rightspellings. This has always happened in English (and other languages, of course)— "chaunte" into "chant," "deliuer" into "deliver." But never before at this rate, I'm sure, and never with this kind of centrality-obliterating fragmentation of authority.

These web-based decentralizations are Vishnuic in a more general way: Prominent cultural, journalistic, and scholarly authorities (like, say, the *New York Times*) have lost some of their centrality, and new and more atomic authorities, with differing points of view—and highly variable reliability—have been created. The speed at which information is made available in turn makes it impossible to keep up with that information, but paradoxically it also makes an ultimately global unity and consciousness seem more possible, in however distant a future. The distinctive communities of every kind now have the potential, for the first time in our species' history, to know about and stay in instant touch with each other.

It's much easier and much harder to keep up. In general, the people I know lean toward a little desperation, lean toward the "harder," more destructive side of the digital Vishnu effect. I do. And a literary friend of mine, young and knowledgeable and the editor of an influential magazine, wrote to me recently, "Except for its use during emergencies and other real crises for individuals or societies, and the instant transmission of critical information, if I could press a button and disinvent the Internet, I would."

The Internet has made it much easier to write this book than it would have been fifty years ago. But because of its mega-omnium-gatherum nature, it has simultaneously, to some extent, made it more difficult. It has subverted the standards that sveltes might have violated more comically—because more violently—fifty years ago.

So, anyway, OK:

67. Cholesteroil

YOU DO THINK of greasy deposits fouling up your aorta when you see the word "cholesterol," so this mistake has a nice logic to it. *Choler,* a word that has historical connections to "cholesterol," meant "bile" in Latin. Bile, the fluid, and one of the four medieval humors (a great rock-band name, but, then, everything is), even looks like oil, of a low grade. If you search around for images of bile, your results remind you that the insides of you are really revolting. Yellow-gray ducts snake around one brown pouch or another and lead to shiitake structures, organs that look like yellow-green chanterelles and have little fluted hats on them. Your liver, a great slab of meat and the bile factory, is where the word "livid" comes from.

It's no wonder that the doctors tell us to avoid cholesterol. Why add grease to the already viscid?

Out into the fresh air, where on a brisk fall day we may catch sight of an old-fashioned brick chimney issuing

68. curly cues

OF SMOKE, AS described in a Facebook post. "Curl" means, more or less, "curl" in all its earlier forms, all the way back to the Proto-Germanic *krusl*. And this svelte is basically just the original cell of "curlicues" dividing. "Cue," on the other hand, gives us more to think about. The theatrical sense of the word probably derives from the Latin *quando,* meaning "when." Shakespeare's folios have their cues as both "Q" and "cue." "Cue" in the pool world started as "queue"—a line or a tail. Or a penis. There is some possibility that the tail of the letter "Q" figures into the meaning of "curlicue."

So you would think that "barbecue," with its smoky overtone, should have some kinship with the "cue" of "curlicue." But no. It's from the Haitian Arawak *barbakoa,* "a framework of sticks," on which the Arawak slept and cured meat, but not at the same time.

You could call the heat of a *barbakoa* or a barbecue

69. ultraviolent radiation —

A SVELTE I found on Reddit. "Ultraviolent" is also, un-surprisingly, the name of a rock band. And it has become a real word by itself, according to *Collins English Dictionary*, though not (yet) in combination with "radiation."

There are two comments that answer Reddit's blog question "Why is ultraviolent radiation so dangerous?"

1.
   - Ubltraviolent [*sic*] radiation means
   - Ultra (extremely)
   - Violent (dangerous to one's cells)
   - Extremely dangerous to one's cells.
   - This is bad because the radiation beats up your cells until they die

2.
   - are you stupid or something? it's in the damn name you dingus. they're ultra violent. those fuckers will kill you if you even make direct eye contact with them.

The accidental discovery that there is a rock band that calls itself Ultraviolent led indirectly to a stock-photo company called Alamy, which offers a picture of American black bears at a

70. garbidge station.

HOW DID THE one lead to the other, you probably haven't wondered. Well, I started thinking about eve-rything being the name of a rock band, so I took "Black Bears" from out of nowhere. It turns out that there is a rock band called the Black Bears, and then I also found the photograph of black bears at a "garbidge station."

Sad to say, "Garbidge" does not appear to be the name of a rock band, unlike (courtesy of the website of the Mem-phis radio station Rock103), among many, many others:

- The Bambi Molesters
- Big Daddy Butt Jelly and the Smooth
- Here, Eat This
- Oedipus and the Mama's Boys
- Snotjet
- The Most Sordid Pies
- Johnny Urinal and the Excreations
- Linoleum Blownapart
- Flopping Bodybags
- Bulimia Blanket
- Pontius Pilate and the Nail Bangers
- Thomas Jefferson Slave Apartments

and yes, and quite famously, "Garbage."

"Linoleum Blownapart" makes it hard to go on. I will go on. To "garbidge." Which was an early variant spelling of "garbage," whose origin seems to have more or less meant itself—refuse, trash—going way back, and may be related, historically and quite logically, to "garble." "-Idge" is a slangy variant form of the suffix "-age," meaning "collection," "amount," "rate" ("dosage," "tonnage"), or "process of" ("coverage," "linkage"), which may account for the appearance of "-age" at the end of "garbage." So much verbiage, I know.

Comical youngsters have toyed with "-idge" and "-age," as in: "Do you have any pennage I could borrow?" "There's too much chairage in this room." "We could hide if only there was some bushidge here."

In the absence of bushidge, here is some more sveltidge: Ultraviolent black bears might kill you and feed on your

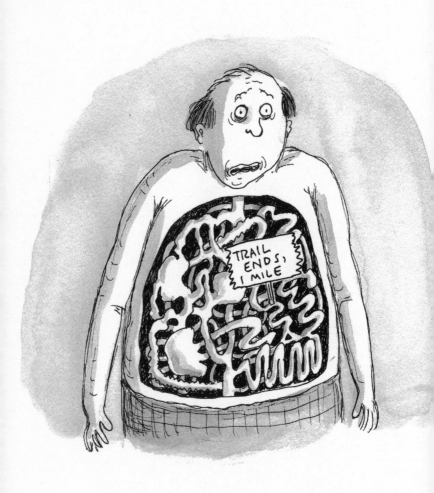

71. end-trails,

ESPECIALLY IF YOU run at them, fail to raise your hands (so they think you're bigger than you are), or make what many authorities refer to as "direct eye contact" with them. (What other kind is there?)

I found "end-trails" for "entrails" on IMDb (the Internet Movie Database), among other places: "He felt he gave it his best shot only to be strung-up by his end-trails." Yet again there is an instinctive sense of correctness lurking like entrails themselves within this svelte. For among your entrails are the end-trails of whatever you eat, your intestines—a word that has the same kind of Latin beginning, *intus,* "within." Whereas hiking "end-trails" couldn't be more external. So there is that kind of contrary fittingness that we've seen before.

There is a myth that humans have twenty-six miles of intestines. Talk about end-trails! But we in fact house twenty-six feet of intestines—plenty enough as far as I'm concerned—before the end of the trail.

End Trails is the name of a rock band. As is

72. Bedside Manor

— AND THAT really ought to do it for rock bands, whose subversive names are beginning to subvert this book.

"Bedside manor" occurs in a social-media endorsement for a veterinarian:

> I want to thank you from the bottom of my heart for the wonderful care that you have given to my baby boy, Simba. With both of his surgeries, the one just done yesterday, you have provided him with the best of care. Your expert medical skills set aside, you have a wonderful bedside manor.

Astonishingly, some of the online letters to vets come from their patients: "Thank you for making my boo-boo go away. Mommy says that she is very thankful of you too! You are the best pet surgeon in the world!" You can also find letters from dogs apologizing to their owners for their misbehavior, and letters from pets in heaven to their owners—they're the most maudlin tripe you can imagine, so why do . . . well, you know—why do they always make me . . . I'll be right back.

"Manner" goes back to the Latin *manus,* for "hand," a natural starting place for a word that means "way of doing things." "Manor" also comes from Latin, *manere,* "to stay or remain," so history once again supports the svelte. I suggest "Bedside Manor" as the name for a nursing home for people who can't get up. Such patients can't run anywhere, physically, but they almost surely can and do

73. run the gammot

OF HUMAN EMOTIONS. "When Hester finally tells Dimmesdale about Chillingworth's true identity, Dimmesdale runs the gammot of human emotion," says a site called Homework Help — some help! — on the subject of Nathaniel Hawthorne's *The Scarlet Letter* (the name of a rock band; can't stop).

"Gammot" *is* a word — for a kind of knife once used in surgery, maybe when the residents of Bedside Manor were young. "Gamut" started in medieval times as the name of the lowest note, G, in the music scale, and later came to designate the entire scale — thus the figurative use of "run the gamut." Try as I may, I can't think of a way in which an obsolete surgical knife and "entire range" can be connected. But I can say, or at least can't not say, that "Gamut" is the name of a rock band. As is

74. Segway,

WHICH, BESIDES BEING the name of a rock band *and* a motorized personal vehicle that makes everyone who rides on it look like a grinning idiot whose car has been impounded, is also sveltian for "segue." Another study guide, called BookRags, tells its unfortunate readers that "a segway into the Introduction is to start it with a little anecdote."

The "way" in the svelte makes perfect sense with "segue," which describes a smooth transition from one part of something—especially, now, conversation or public speaking—to another, a transition usually without a pause. In Italian, the musical notation *segue,* from its Latin root *sequi,* means "now follows." (The same root has given us "sequel.") The trade name for the ludicrous motorized personal vehicle, I have to admit, is, retroactively, what makes the svelte at all sveltic. Well, not quite. Because the "seg" portion of "segue" and "Segway"—and "sequel" and "segment," "sequester" and "sequitur" (but not, as I'd hoped, "sequin")—comes from the Latin *seccare,* "to cut off." Which gives us another of those graceful etymological paradoxes. Buried inside a smooth transition there has to be a cutoff, however indiscernible.

Segues have been among the most challenging aspects of writing this book. Surely you knew that, from noticing the lameness of some of them. So let's give them a rest and stay, with regard to segues,

75. above approach,

AS A CHRISTIAN BLOGGER said about the way he lives his life: "I know I sin everyday but i strive to live in a manner that is above approach."

"Approach" and "reproach" come from the same Latin source, *propiare*, "to come nearer." According to some etymologists, the Latin suffix *-re*, "opposite of," in combination with *prope-*, "near," gives us "reproach," the opposite of coming near or being friendly. In fact, creating an antagonistic distance.

In a certain way, if your conduct is above reproach, it's also above approach. That is, if your standards and behavior are above approach, no one can get near enough to compromise them. Still, I have to admit that the two words are not what a novel called *Fish Stories* said of three men who came into a bar. They were

76. dead wringers

FOR JOSEPH STALIN, Franklin Roosevelt, and Winston Churchill.

"Dead" makes some sense, and not only because it's part of the origin phrase; "wringers" makes sense only sveltically. If that. If you wring something out, you're left with its essence, so you can think of a wringer as someone who gets the basic nature of whatever it is that's being wrung, except necks, maybe. So a dead wringer might be the ghost of a laundry maid in the process of restoring a garment to its original, dryer, more normal state. A reach, but there's something there.

And a dead ringer is someone who exactly imitates the basic nature or demeanor or appearance of someone else, thus conveying his essence to the people he's trying to fool. "Dead" in this sense — "absolute, utter" — started in the late sixteenth century, evidently because nothing is utterer or more absolute than death.

"Ringer" is more interesting, because in the sense of "a substitute," it first appeared in reference to racehorses that looked like other racehorses and were surreptitiously substituted for their look-alikes because they were faster (or slower), so that those in the crooked know could more easily win bets. It worked both ways, as long as you knew that Jolly Rancher, say, wasn't the horse that other bettors thought it was.

But wait—why "ringer"? After the rounded nature of racetracks. Or maybe—or maybe also—because, etymologists have suggested, of the phrase "to ring changes," which applies specifically to improvisations—substitutes for straight melodies—on church bells.

I will resist the temptation to tell you that Dead Ringer *and* Dead Wringers are both names of rock bands, the latter being the backup band for, naturally, George Washingmachine, at the recent Boot and Flogger reunion party.

Human wringers may well be the kinds of people who also try to

77. wrangle an invitation

TO, SAY, the White House—as a website said that the Malaysian prime minister tried to do some years ago. "Wangle" and "wrangle" are etymologically distant, but they turn out to be historically and definitionally closer than you might have guessed. *Webster's Dictionary of English Usage* has it that "wangle," meaning "to obtain in an indirect or sly way," started in about 1900. The same source goes on to say that sometimes "wrangle" is used in the same way, as in "wrangle a cheap ticket," but usually it means "to argue or engage in controversy." The "obtain" sense of "wrangle" did not evolve through confusion with "wangle," however, because, according to *Webster's,* "wrangle" meant "to obtain by arguing or bargaining" in the early seventeenth century, well before "wangle" appeared in the language. This usage had nearly vanished until recently, though, and its reappearance was probably influenced by "wangle." The "obtain" definition of "wangle" is now more common than that of "wrangle," but, the usage dictionary says, "both are considered standard."

Both are considered standard? *Both are considered standard?* Why, then, this svelte is nothing but an

78. imposter.

OMG, "IMPOSTER" MAY BE another svelte "impostor,"
since many sources say that both spellings are now acceptable. Oh, well, "imposter" looks like a mistake to me,
and so the real etymologists will probably ring my neck.
They both come from the English variant form "im-" of
the Latin prefix *in-*, meaning "not," as in "invalid," "inau-
dible," etc., and *ponere*, "to put or place." So, like a ringer,
a horse that is in fact an impostor, when you think about
it, is a horse that is in place of another horse. On second
thought, can horses properly be called frauds of any sort,
since they can't know they are?

By now you can certainly guess without my telling you
what the Imposters *and* the Impostors also are . . . That's
right—each member, we hope, is what the sociologist
Simon Frith's book *Performing Rites* quite seriously called
Bruce Springsteen, namely, a "skilled

79. rock and role

PERSON." LIKE MORE than a few other sveltes, "role" and "roll" are amphibious. From the website Quora: "How do genetics play a roll in the failure of joints as one enters old age?"

Plus, it happens that both words started with the same French word — *rôle*, figuratively "the part played by a person in his or her life," and literally "a roll of paper." The latter transfer may have happened because actors' parts were once written on rolls of paper.

Can we just back up here and appreciate "roll in the failure of joints," as that's the very problem — there's more creaking and scraping and less and less roll in the joints as we age. And, for that matter, what, besides a musician, is a rock performer if not a role player, I ask you.

The same Quora site lists questions related to the one about the "roll" of genetics in the failure of joints. One of these questions is "I look 3 years older than my age. What does it mean?" A lot if you're two, is my answer, and not much if you're seventy-five. (Marshall Brickman published a humor piece in *The New Yorker* in which he described a 115-year-old jazz trumpet player as having "the lucidity of a man fifteen years his junior.")

Like selfies to a blogger, at seventy-five, age discrimination is

80. something that really gets my gander up.

YES, WHENEVER he thinks I'm being shut out of something on account of my years, my gander rises from his slumber and squawks in protest.

Neither "gander" nor "dander" appears to have an interesting lineage. Some etymological authorities bewilderingly find no connection between "dander" and "dandruff." Other sources do.

Ganders do raise their long necks in alarm or when threatened, so the mistake makes conceptual sense. It says here and there that Newfoundland's Gander River, after which Gander Lake and the town of Gander are named, got its name from the multiplicity of geese in the neighborhood. Shouldn't these sources say "ganders"? I guess "goose" comprehends "gander"—after all, sauce for the one is sauce for the other. It is nice in this avian connection that the Gander airfield has played such an important part in military- and commercial-flight history. As the facility says of itself, in the history section of its website, FlyGander:

Gander's beginnings date back to 1936 when the construction of the international airport began in earnest ... A few years later the airfield had four paved runways—the largest airport in the world at the time ...

By the outbreak of war in September 1939, Gander was ready for civil operations. The value of a functioning airport in such a strategic position was unique ... The airport at Gander became the main staging point for the movement of Allied aircraft to Europe during World War II ... In November 1940, Captain D.C.T. Bennett left Gander for Europe, leading the first fleet of seven Lockheed Hudson bombers across the Atlantic during the Battle of Britain. More than 20,000 North American–built fighters and heavy bombers would follow ...

In 1942, the Newfoundland Government handed over the control of the airport to the Canadian Government and it became a military airfield, with a continuous delivery of planes to the war zone. In 1945, the Newfoundland government took over control of the airport again.

The elevation involved in getting one's gander up harmonizes not only with the aptronymic male geese and the name of the town and airport, but Howard Hughes's ill-fated World War II all-wood transport plane, the *Spruce Goose*.

Hughes was famously a recluse and a hypochondriac. Hypochondria has gone viral on the web — so many opportunities for public anxieties about medical matters, such as,

81. When I wake up I have to hack up mukis.

NOT A SVELTE, you say? "Mukis" isn't a real word? Don't get your gander up. *Muka*, plural *mukis*, is Lower Sorbian for "powder." And anyway, this svelte candidate was sent to me by a doctor on whose close attention my life may depend, so you will understand why it is included. Beyond that, the half-staccato, half-slimy sound of the sentence appealed to me, in an unappealing way.

Another medical puzzlement:

82. Can the Gaul Bladder Envelope the Liver?

THERE IS NO answer on steadyhealth.com, but I would say: Only in France could this happen. And only when Charles de Gall led the country. You will also find online here and there "onmitigated gaul." There's no connection between "gall" and "Gaul," though one day, a Gaul in Paris, actually smoking a Gauloise, I swear, had the gall to engage me in the following dialogue:

GAUL: You Amerikainz—you know nussing about ze politiques.
ME: Well, we've had the same government for more than two hundred years.
GAUL: You see what I mean!

"Envelope" for "envelop"—not worth discussing. But in the same international/bodily secretion connection, myhealthtips.com offers

83. Home Remedies to Treat Flem in Throat. (Cf. No. 81.)

"FLEM" IS NOT only the first name of the unpleasant Faulkner character Flem Snopes, it's also a shortened word for a Flemish person—a Belgian from the northern area of Flanders. Don't you wonder how such proper nouns change so much when they become adjectives? Oxford, Oxonian. Cambridge, Cantabrigian. Flanders, Flemish. I think I could tell you, now, but this isn't the time or place.

If you have a Flem lodged in your throat, home remedies are not going to help. If you have heard Flemish spoken, though, you know that like its parent, Dutch, it can sound a little hawky, or

84. gutteral.

"WHAT VESSELS ARE seen traveling just outside of the gutteral pouch wall?" yet another imperfect veterinary forum asks. Well, none, it is to be hoped. *Staying still outside* the guttural pouch, which is found in most equids (horses, etc.), are the external and internal carotid arteries.

There is no etymological connection between "guttural" and "gutter," surprisingly. But unsurprisingly, in Latin, *guttur* meant "throat," the beginning of the "elementary" canal. And *gutta* meant "drop" (of water), which, when it got together with other drops, formed a derivational stream that led to "gutter." So there is a strong imagistic connection between the two words. Let's not forget "gutta-percha" (from Malay: *gĕtah*, sap, latex; *pĕrcha*, the tree producing this substance), a plastic-like material that has been used for many things, from insulation to golf balls to root canals.

I fear that svelte may

85. pail in comparison

TO OTHERS — as a sports column said of the champion fighter Floyd Mayweather's offensive boxing skills vs. his defense. It's getting late in the day, and maybe it just seems a bit pale. There is a pail in a boxer's corner, at least the movie palooka's corner, isn't there, and if you think of a pail as often being the repository for something discarded, something used up, the svelte begins to recover a little color.

After the fight a couple of years ago against Manny Pacquiao—a lackluster affair according to all observers, including this one—disparagements of Mayweather started

86. spreading like wildflowers.

ONCE AGAIN WE have a svelte spreading so rapidly—
the Eggcorn Forum has found 352 Google hits for the
phrase—that it threatens to become correct, or at least
"correct." Wildflowers and wildfires both spread, of
course—the one benignly, even prettily, and slowly,
for the most part,* the other quickly and threateningly.
But you can easily see where the confusion came from.
Maybe we can and should reserve the sense-making
"wildflowers" comparison for nice spreading phenomena, like, well, kayaking**, and retain the "wildfire" trope,
which is now used for good and bad alike, exclusively for
bad ones, especially illnesses that are accompanied by
fevers.

---

* "for the most part" because wildflowers, like wildfires, sometimes
have their own destructive and invasive behavior. My uncle, Frederick Engels Menaker [sic], planted *Aegopodium podagraria* L. as a ground
cover at his house in Massachusetts, which is now my family's house.
Aegopodium podagraria L. is also commonly called ground elder, herb
gerard, bishop's weed, goutweed, gout wort, and snow-in-the-moun-
tain, and sometimes called English masterwort and wild masterwort.
It has one of the worst horticultural reputations going. Gardeners'

adjectives about it include "invasive," "insidious"—well, wait, here's part of what the blog of one gardener, Carole Sevilla Brown, has to say about bishop's weed:

> It wreaks havoc in moist, partly shaded woodlands and disturbed areas. It forms a dense mat that prohibits other plants from establishing . . . This trait is especially harmful in natural wooded areas where it outcompetes native plants. Because of this, many native woodland plants are now highly endangered.
>
> I've been attempting to rid my property of this plant since 2001 when I first moved in. It feels like a losing battle because the weed always returns with a vengeance, especially after the rain. We pull, and we pull, and then we pull some more. But it always comes back.
>
> That's because Bishop Weed not only spreads by seed, it also spreads by underground runners. If you're pulling but don't get every last piece of those runners out of the ground, it will pop up again almost immediately . . .
>
> It is banned for sale in Connecticut, Massachusetts, and Vermont, and is considered a noxious pest from Eastern Canada to Georgia and into the midwest, plus is invasive in the Pacific Northwest.

That this weed is banned from sale, a controlled botanical, makes me envision black-market peddlers, like drug dealers, hawking their noxious rhizomes on roadsides outside Brattleboro. At our farmhouse, the bishop's weed is slowly taking over our lawn. This predator stands vigil at the borders, and if we turn our backs for a second, when we turn back around it has occupied a couple more centimeters. We can almost hear it jeering our efforts at control.

In this regenerative talent, bishop's weed resembles that tiny animal, friend to many biology students, the hydra, which undergoes morphallaxis (tissue regeneration) when injured or severed and is non-senescent—biologically immortal! The hydra does not senesce.

These examples of animal and vegetable tenacity correspond to the way words, and word errors, grow and invade correct language and often can't be killed. The wrong way occupies the right way's territory, and grammarians' and lexicographers' efforts to control or eliminate it fail—as the analysis of invasive mistakes back at No. 37 makes clear. The difference is that the sveltes that actually become accepted do so because they work. They don't destroy but in a way "evolve" other words and create new usages. "Grow like wildflowers" adds something to the language, and like many other sveltes (and unlike bishop's weed) probably doesn't, for now, threaten the original verbal ecology—"wildfire."

That word back there, "correspond," reminds me, ever so distantly, of a book called The *Elizabethan World Picture,* by E.M.W. Tillyard, a standard text about the culture that surrounded, among others, Shakespeare. It argues that the era was more nearly a continuation of the medieval worldview than a steppingstone to modernity. In it, Tillyard discusses the Elizabethans' concept of "Correspondences," summed up here in an excellent study guide posted by the English Department at Weston High School in Massachusetts:

Key Concepts:

- Correspondence between divine being and sun (and "son" in the Christian imagery Shakespeare uses)
- Macrocosm and body politic—the connection between the state of the universe and the condition of the political state
- Macrocosm and microcosm—the correspondence between

the state of the universe and the condition of an individual (including specific correspondences such as the sun and the heart, water and blood, etc.)

- Body politic and microcosm—the correspondence between the condition of the political state and the condition of an individual (especially the state's ruler)
- Metaphor v. equivalence. (What we see as a metaphor, the Elizabethans saw as "equivalent." It's not simply that the body of a king is a metaphor for the country. They actually are equivalent, each corresponding to the other on a different plane of existence.)

Happy reading!

At the start of this study guide, the faculty writes:

Shakespeare often builds the imagistic structure of his plays using the idea of "Correspondences." You might think of the main idea as "Everything is a metaphor for everything else," though, as the end of the chapter suggests, it's more than just a metaphor.

** "Kayaking" is all that came to me as a nice spreading phenomenon. I don't know why. Surely there are countless other nice spreading phenomena, though for my taste, kale, quinoa, and hummus are not among them.

In fact, they are so noisome to me that they remind me of this quote from a book called *Bulimia: Hunger for Freedom:*

87. I was a skid-roe bulimic.

NEITHER "ROE" NOR "row" (in the sense of a line) has a colorful etymological past. Their antecedents, in Old Norse, Sanskrit, etc., meant more or less what they mean today. "Skid," on the other hand, offers some texture. "On the skids" probably derives from loggers' quarters in Seattle in the nineteenth century, since roads there consisted of skids—boards whose purpose was to facilitate moving heavy objects—laid down to form paths over mud and muck. In fact, the original phrase was probably "skid road," making "skid row" a svelte that has completely bishop's-weeded its predecessor. The meaning became deteriorative, going from loggers' quarters, to where migrants in general lived, to bums' habitat.

"Skid" probably comes from Old Norse, *skið*, meaning "stick." It came as a pleasant even if logical surprise to me to learn that "ski" is historically related to "skid."

People who live on skid row usually don't have to file revenue reports for the

88. physical year,

NOT TO MENTION the fiscal one. North Carolina A&T State University assures its faculty, about insurance, that "the coverage is automatic and state agencies complete a self-audit at the beginning of the physical year." As far as I can tell, they mean "fiscal."

"Fiscal" comes from the Latin *fiscus*, "purse," and, more primally, "basket made of twigs in which money was kept." So you see. About where "fiscal" comes from, I mean. What you may not see is the sveltic connection between "physical" and "fiscal," so here is the nut of it: Some organizations deliberately use the term "physical year" to mean "calendar year"—the calendar, at least sometimes, being a physical object. They do this to distinguish it from the fiscal year, which is often *not* January 1 through December 31 but a different twelve-month period.

So, in a way, "physical year" is essentially one of those errors (with approaching validation) that connect with their correct spellings by a species of opposition. Because "physical year" evokes weather and a material calendar, whereas "fiscal year" is stubbornly, antagonistically abstract, not tied to any *Playboy* babes or version of meteorological phenomena or sun phases.

Weather: When you have indoor work to do, a rainy day can come as a

89. blessing in the skies,

WHICH IS WHAT one Golden State Warrior called his teammate's injury on the team's website during the NBA playoffs in 2007. (Because it made him, the blessed one, play harder and better?) Since many religions' doctrines would have it that the skies, the heavens, are where blessings come from, the svelte has that resonance.

You would guess that "disguise" must originate in Latin, somewhere back there, because of the Latin-looking prefix. But no. Both prefix and main part of the word come from the Old French *disguiser,* "to change one's appearance." "Guise" started with the Proto-Germanic *wisson,* "appearance, manner." The oldest sense of "disguise" was the state of being put out of one's usual appearance or manner, as in "disguised with liquor."

"Bless" also started out Proto-Germanically, with *blodison,* "to hallow with blood, mark with blood," from *blotham,* "blood."

And "sky"? For a long time its Old Norse and Proto-Indo-European roots meant "cloud," "cover," or "hide." Like a disguise!

So there you have it, troubling though it may be to think of blood raining down from above.

In Kerala, India, *National Geographic* reported a blood-red rain falling during the monsoon season. Freaky video. You could apply the cliché, however lamely, that this rain was a horse of a different color. But if you were thebigadventure1 blogspot, you would say it was a

90. horse of a different collar.

WHAT CAME TO MIND when I first saw this svelte was the now-outlawed horse-collar tackle—a foul in football that consists of a defensive player grabbing a runner by the back of his jersey, especially near a shoulder, and twisting it, and thus him, to the ground. Of course a horse collar is a real thing—you put it around the horse's neck and attach traces to it, to be able to hitch him up to a load. And my guess is that the person who committed this svelte had that compound noun hitched up to the horse in his mind.

"Collar" started out as an old word for "neck," logically enough. You know, wait a second. "Horse of different collar" makes total sense, since horses wear collars and there are different kinds for different hauling purposes: the Kay collar, the Quarter Sweeny, the Half Sweeny, and the Full Sweeny.

I had this svelte in mind after "blessing in the skies" because, like "sky," "color" grew from a root that meant "cover" or "hide"—the Old Latin *colos*, originally "covering" or "concealment."

In a post on Historically Speaking, an excellent site about idiom sources, Elyse Bruce points out that in Act 2,

Scene 3 of *Twelfth Night,* in which Maria schemes with Sir Andrew and Toby Belch against Malvolio, we hear:

MARIA: My purpose is, indeed, a horse of that colour.
SIR ANDREW: And your horse now would make him
    an ass.

"Horse of that color" appears to imply that "horse of a different color" may have been an idiom already in use. And "horse of that color" predominated for a considerable time as an expression used to convey similarity. "Horse of a different color," a play on words already metaphorical and maybe even clichéd, appears to have started galloping around seriously at the beginning of the twentieth century.

Speaking of quadrupeds, a character in a novel called *Manhunting in Montana* describes her situation as being

91. like a puppy on a string.

"PUPPY" AND "PUPPET" come from the same French root—*poupée,* for "doll" or "toy." The image that "puppy on a string" summons up is a little kid using a string as a leash for a toy dog. In fact, "puppy on a string" makes more sense altogether than "puppet on a string," because it's marionettes that are generally on strings. (By the way, "marionette" may well have started with the name of Jesus's mother.) But that hasn't kept "puppet on a string" from becoming a trope for someone who is at someone else's beck and call. Or the title of two popular songs, both from the 1960s.

Nursing homes employ dogs as "comfort animals." Maybe these places should also consider using the centerpiece of the dish mentioned in this review of a restaurant in Venice:

92. My main meal was spaghetti with cuddle-fish sauce.

BEING A FOOD-AS-FUEL kind of person, I find any kind of writing about eating, even simple reporting like this, at least faintly hilarious—like most writing about sex. To bedeck these basic functions with words, especially elegant or lyrical ones, is like trying to make music out of the animal noises so variously transliterated, or just literated, in No. 62.

"Cuttle" comes from an Old Norse word for "bag" or, like the Aztec *ahuacatl*, "testicle." They are remarkably ugly and improbable-looking animals, are cuttlefish. So to think of getting cozy with them is kind of revolting.

"Cuddle" has a muddy background: either the obsolete English word "cull" ("to embrace," related to "collar") or the Middle English *couth*, "known, familiar" and thus "at ease with." In either case, "cuddle-fish" once again presents us with the dissonant appropriateness of many other sveltes.

The "cuddle-fish," being evidently soft and affectionate, is surely the

93. pillow of his community

94. "a pillow of strength"

FOR OTHER FISH SPECIES.

Believe it or not, No. 94 threatens to join the *OED* list of mistakes that happen often enough to become one of those damned "valid alternatives." You can find pillows of communities and strength in many obituaries generated by funeral homes. You begin to think that the recumbence of their clientele has had a linguistic effect on the funeral directors' vocabulary.

Both "pillow" and "pillar" are fairly direct descendants of their (respectively) Germanic and Latin ancestors. Substituting the first for the second once again shows that when it comes to sveltes, opposites frequently attract. But in this case, paradoxically, the opposites also are not only opposite but sort of synonymous. That is, as a pillar offers metaphorical benefit to his or her community, so does its pillow. The one, strength. The other, rest.

Finding these marriages of opposites

95. never seizes to amaze me,

AS A FACEBOOK post, worthy of quoting at some length, said of the morning rituals it attributed to many of us:

> Never seizes to amaze me and it continually amazes me at the abuse most people subject themselves to at the start of each day. They will look at themselves in the mirror in the morning and say: fat face, big legs, huge stomach, fat ass.

"Cease" comes from the Latin *cedere*, "to go away, withdraw" and so is closely related to "cede." "Seize" started out as the Old English *secan*, "to search for, pursue, long for." So the will of wanting (*secan*) has become the deed of taking ("seizing").

If something seizes you—your imagination, say—it also causes you to cease anything else you may be doing or thinking about. So you could say, "It *always* seizes to amaze me" and make a little sense. So yet again, two words, one mistakenly used for the other, "seize" and "cease," are on the same continuum but at opposite ends.

At very close to the same end of the sveltish continuum, we have the website singersroom.com saying,

96. The Janet Jackson . . . halftime performance mishap . . . has been edged in stone as a historical television incident.

"EDGED" AND "ETCHED" make immediate visual sense as close kin, surely because etching is generally done with sharp tools, tools with edges. Their etymologies devolve into Proto-Germanic, Old Frisian, Old Saxon, Middle Dutch, Dutch, Old Norse, and others. Hiding somewhere in back of "etch" is the Old High German *azzon*, meaning "to give to eat, cause to bite, feed." Etching instruments do indeed take "bites" out of the material they work on, just as edgers chop away messy lawn borders.

That wardrobe malfunction turned into

97. a fine fettle of fish

(UNDER THESE CIRCUMSTANCES, maybe cuddle-fish). This alliterative svelte occurred, without an apparent wink, on Yahoo Answers. And yet again we have something of an oxymoronic suitability of an error in relation to its correct form. "Fine kettle of fish" carries with it the sense of a complicated problem or predicament, whereas "fettle" has strong positive connotations.

"Fettle" goes back to and replicates the Middle English verb *fettle*, "to make ready, prepare, arrange," so if you're in fine fettle, you're well arranged. Gerard Manley Hopkins writes, of a blacksmith,

> *When thou at the random grim forge, powerful*
> *amidst peers,*
> *Didst fettle for the great grey drayhorse his bright*
> *and battering sandal!*

And "kettle" winds forward from the usual Proto suspects to the Latin *catinus*—"bowl, pot, dish."

A fine kettle of verbal fish are the following, svelte grouping:

98, 99, 100, and 100+.
Breech, broach, and breach.
And, come to think of it, brooch.

"I LOVE TALKING dirty during sex—but how can I breech the subject with my boyfriend?" asks some hoyden on Reddit. She may have already, since one meaning of "breech," from an Old German root, is the aperture of the buttocks. (Thus, by the way, "breeches.")

On bluelight.org we find more "br"-related sexual content:

> Every time I try to breach the subject [of sex] with my wife, she gets furious. I have no idea why. If anyone who can shed some light upon this subject cares to share, it would be a great help. Peace.

"To breach" literally means "to make a gap and break through." In fact, its Proto-Indo-European form, *bregh,* means "to break." In this usage, it's not so far from the more correct verb "broach." Which has also come to be accepted as an alternate spelling for "brooch."

These four words are like quadruplets, always being

mistaken for one another, used as verbs when they are nouns and vice versa, related etymologically, all to some extent having to do with openings. A "brooch" is a kind of jewelry, fastened with a pin, but a family-law firm has dragged it into this "br" family when it said, "Many couples hesitate to enter into prenuptial agreements or even brooch the subject."

I saved this covey of confusions for last in order to breach, broach, and brooch the subject of ending this book—the final breech. But I will do so with a bonus from a pertinent Facebook post, which said that no one should buy books from anywhere but

101. a brick and mortal store.

I ADMIRE THE idealism here, but I'm afraid that that particular e-cow is pretty well out of the interbarn. "Brick and mortar" conveys a kind of solid, material reality that pixels can't achieve. And the stores themselves offer such excellent shelter from the impersonally imperfect storm of the e-tailers that ship your books to your own home. What in this regard is so great about your own home? As good books take us out of ourselves, brick-and-mortar stores take us out of our nests. It's true, though, that pixels offer many advantages, not least among them portability, and that anything like a full retreat from electronic books is impossible now.

The comparison that comes to mind here is vinyl records vs. CDs and other digital formats. There has been a resurgence of LPs, especially among young people, but Pandora and Spotify and other music-streaming services will continue to thrive. Convenient!

"Mortal," derived from the Latin root denoting death ("mortal wound"), is also a synonym for "human being" ("What fools these mortals be!"), and so the word contains within it not only our being but our universal ultimate fate—nonbeing. "Brick-and-mortal" stores are therefore for actual, live human beings to be alive in. Whereas the cyberspace in which dwell e-books and online commerce presents a kind of paradoxical emptiness, precisely because of its seeming immortality. And as we have seen, a mortar—the weapon—destroys, whereas mortar—the substance—builds.

In many cases, brick-and-mortar bookstores are proving all too mortal. As with most if not all the sveltes listed here, there is indeed poetry, elegiac, in this mistake.

AFTERWORD

LANGUAGE IS A NET that we cast over the world. It helps us catch the world, but it also separates us from it, just as catching a netful of fish makes them ours, in a way, but also differs radically from swimming among them and knowing them that way. Language also represents the world, and our minds tell us that the words we use and the senses that bring the world into our minds are apprehending and understanding the world.

They're not. The world—reality, whatever that happens to be—is recondite. It stands before us like some silent Himalaya. We scramble around it, we can even reach its summit (great poetry), but its full, true nature remains obdurate against the kind of comprehensive understanding that our consciousness—that supremely accomplished charlatan—tells us we have. Animals—most if not all of them almost certainly lacking anything like human consciousness and its preeminent production, human-style language—must know, or at least must experience, the world more directly than we do. No naming intervenes between their experience of the world and the world itself. Sometimes I imagine they live as in a permanent dream. Or a permanent experiential poem.

So all our words are bastards fathered by a reality that knows and cares nothing about them. But, as with the string and openings of a net, or all the cells in our bodies, all words, in every language and across languages, have to do with one another, and all mistakes relate to their correctnesses and to each other. To savor the humor and meaning of errors is at least implicitly to acknowledge the universality of our basic existential bafflement. When we see Charlie Chaplin slip on a banana peel, our laughter, if we have any decency, results not from watching some poor schmo slip on a banana peel, but ultimately from the recognition that we are all poor schmos, set down here on the banana peel of life with some occasional rhyme but no reason.

In more senses than the obvious one, to err is human. And often funny. And, always, meaningful.

And so dusk has fallen on the African svelte. Time to end this safari. Our quarry has been caught and is herewith released, back into the endless fields of our wonderful written language. If you keep your eye out, you will find new sveltic species on your own, waiting to be admired and understood for the gorgeously piebald creatures they are.

ACKNOWLEDGMENTS

1. James Gleick,

ace encourager, champion svelte provider, good friend. "James" goes back, mysteriously, through "Jacob" to the Hebrew verb *aqab,* "heel grasper." That's what it says, somewhere.

No less essential to whatever merit this weird book may have was

2. Jenna Johnson,

enthusiastic editor, warden of precision, scourge of cuteness, demander of detail. "Jenna" may have once meant "little bird." Listen to what she tells you. As you should to anything

3. Esther Newberg,

my agent provocateur, champion of authors, says, however briefly. She once congratulated me on a book contract and then reminded me, with some glee, "Now all you have to do is write it!"

"Esther" derives, appropriately, from the Persian *sitareh*, "star." In the same gorgeous constellation you will find

4. Roz Chast and Billy Collins,

illustrator and foreworder, respectively, whose names are virtually their own exegeses. (They have something to do, respectively, with horses and "victory.") The lodestar here is

5. Katherine Bouton,

my wife and *Svelte*'s dedicatee, who suffered patiently and supportively as I cruised and occasionally cursed my way through the writing of this book. "Katherine" descends originally from an ancient word for "pure," and "Bouton" at least in part from "button," and from her—whom we should thank for the idea of this book's enumerative nature—and me descend our kids,

6. William and Elizabeth,

both of whom tolerate and occasionally even seem to appreciate my jokes, and both of whose names, to me, mean "love" and "pride." And then there is a

7. whole bunch of other crucial publishing people at Houghton Mifflin Harcourt —

Bruce Nichols, honcho; Stephanie Kim, super-publicist; Pilar Garcia-Brown, the best at what she does and with a name to kill for; Katrina Kruse; Lori Glazer; Ben Hyman; and all the other good HMHers, especially Larry Cooper, manuscript editor nonparallel. Their invaluable inside assistance has been complemented from the outside by

8. a "pluthora" of scholarly and/or online expertise,

most prominently the *Oxford English Dictionary*; its abbreviational cousin the *Online Etymology Dictionary*; the Language Log, which is a weblog run by the University of Pennsylvania and overseen by Mark Liberman (who coined the term "eggcorn") and Geoffrey K. Pullum, and which, on the day of this writing, made fun of Bernie Sanders for a tweet that refers to nouns as adjectives; the Egg-corn Forum—a kind of outgrowth of the Language Log—originated and brilliantly supervised by Chris Waigl; *Word Origins and How We Know Them: Etymology for Everyone* by Anatoly Liberman (Oxford University Press, 2009); *Philosophy in the Flesh: The Embodied Mind and Its Challenge to Western Thought* by George Lakoff and Mark Johnson (Basic Books, 1999); "More about Metaphor" by Max Black, an article in the publication *dialectica* (2007); *The Oxford Companion to the English Language,* edited by Tom McArthur (Oxford University Press, 1992); *The Body in Question* by Gregory Dawes (Brill, 1998); *Etymologicon: A Circular Stroll Through the Hidden Connections of the English Language* by Mark Forsyth (Berkley reprint edition, 2012), a book that marries wit and erudition in the most excellent way; *The Secret Life of Words: How English Became English* by Henry Hitchings (Farrar, Straus & Giroux, 2008), just superb; *Dictionary of Word Origins: Histories of More Than 8,000 English-Language Words* by John Ayto (Arcade, 1990); verbotomy .com; englishstackexchange.com; alphadictionary.com; wordorigins.org (particularly good); and many others, including, most importantly, those of us—surely close to all of us—who commit sveltes and so, however unknowingly, add bright threads of poetry and complexity to this gorgeous monstrosity English, a language spoken and written with invention and singular clarity by

9. Mary Grace, Robert Menaker, Thearetha Rogowski, Frederick Engels Menaker, and Samuel Hynes,

my parents.

> **parent (n.)**
> early 15c. (late 12c. as a surname), from Old French *parent* "father, parent, relative, kin" (11c.), from Latin *parentem* (nominative *parens*) "father or mother, ancestor," noun use of present participle of *parere* "bring forth, give birth to, produce," from PIE root **pere-* (1) "to bring forth" (see *pare*). Began to replace native *elder* after c. 1500.   —*Online Etymology Dictionary*